The Capsule

Walter Hampel

Restoring The Core

Acknowledgments

There are several people to thank for their contributions to this book prior to publication. Rebecca Ensign (goldleafpress.com) was the editor. Several individuals did a pre-publication review. Those were my wife, Julie, Dr. David Hodge, Michelle Hodge, Steven Seaton, and Anthony Veltri Jr.

Bible Versions

Unless otherwise noted, Scripture quotations are from the ESV®Bible (The Holy Bible, English Standard Version®), copyright© 2001 by Crossway Bibles, a publishing ministry of Good News Publishers. Used by permission. All rights reserved.

Cover Credit

Cover Photo: Earth and Moon taken from the Lunar Reconnaissance Orbiter October 12, 2015; Image Credit: NASA/Goddard/Arizona State University

To my grandchildren Ezekiel, Ezra, and all who may follow,
wonderful reminders of why this book was written:

So even to old age and gray hairs,
O God, do not forsake me,
until I proclaim your might to another generation,
your power to all those to come.

Psalm 71:18

Contents

Introduction

When you pray, you are not to be like the hypocrites; for they love to stand and pray in the synagogues and on the street corners so that they may be seen by men. Truly I say to you, they have their reward in full. But you, when you pray, go into your inner room, close your door and pray to your Father who is in secret, and your Father who sees what is done in secret will reward you. Matthew 6:5-6 NASB

In the late 1960s and early 1970s, the United States embarked on Project Apollo. It was created in response to President John Kennedy's challenge to land men on the Moon and return them safely to Earth before the end of the decade of the 1960s.1 By the end of 1969, two Apollo missions had successfully landed on the Moon and brought their crews safely back to Earth. Four other landing missions followed in 1971 and 1972.

Each Apollo mission had a three-man crew. For the lunar-landing missions, several days after leaving Earth, two tandem spacecraft entered into an orbit around the Moon. Two of the astronauts would descend to the surface of the Moon in their Lunar Excursion Module. The third astronaut would remain in the mother ship (known as the Command Module). The third astronaut's mission was to keep that spacecraft in lunar orbit until his fellow astronauts returned.

What happened with the lone astronaut in the orbiting Apollo capsule has intrigued me. At the time of this writing, seven men in history have had the opportunity to experience isolation on a scale that can be hard for us to imagine. Their experience is the basis for a pattern and mindset that can be adapted as an approach to your devotional time with Christ.

Each Apollo mission involved numerous Command Module orbits of the Moon. For about half of each orbit around the Moon (47 minutes on average for Apollo 11)[2], the Apollo Command Module was behind the Moon in relation to Earth. When that happened, the Moon blocked any radio signals sent between the Command Module and Mission Control on Earth. Even the astronauts on the surface of the Moon would not be able to contact their fellow astronaut in the Command Module during that part of the orbit. The lone astronaut, during that time of the orbit on the far side of the Moon, was the most isolated human being in existence.

As of the early 21st century, the holder of the Guinness World record for the most isolated human ever was Al Worden, the Command Module pilot on the Apollo 15 mission in 1971. The orbit of the Command Module put Worden at the furthest distance that one human has ever been from another. The two closest humans (his fellow astronauts on the surface of the Moon) were, at points, several thousand miles away from Worden. The rest of humanity was over 238,000 miles away back on Earth.

Once the Command Module's orbit took it from behind the Moon, the loss-of-signal ended and communication with Mission Control on Earth was restored. On every orbit, the Command Module pilot experienced what author Cal Newport refers to in his book *Digital Minimalism* as a "cycle of solitude and connection." [3] I believe this cycle offers you a pattern for living your life in the presence of Christ for there are times when you not only should, but must, be away from others.

Why do we do what we do?

The Bible repeatedly shows us that our outward actions may be in conflict with our inner motivations. Proverbs 16:2 reminds us that *"all the ways of a man are clean in his own sight, But the LORD weighs the motives."*

In His time on Earth, the Lord Jesus called out those whose inner motivations and outward actions did not line up. He called them hypocrites. In classical Greek theater, a hypocrite was an actor portraying a role. That actor pretended to be one person but was really someone else. This description fits many of the religious practitioners of first-century Israel.

One example of this can be found in their prayer practices. What was intended to be a time of private prayer became a display of prayer performed in the midst of a crowd. Such a zealous person would ensure that they would be in a crowd during the time of prayer. Albert Barnes, in his commentary on Matthew 6, further explains the matter. Public prayer was not the issue.

> The Jews were much in the habit of praying in public places. At certain times of the day they always offered their prayers. Wherever they were, they suspended their employment and paid their devotions . . . It seems, also, that they [the hypocrites] sought publicity, and regarded it as proof of great piety.4

The Inner Room

The ultimate goal of public prayer for these hypocrites was to be seen by the crowd as a zealous follower of God. Yet, the Lord Jesus called for His followers to do the exact opposite.

The Capsule

Rather than being seen by others, Christ's followers were to offer their prayers privately, not for an open and public display. They were to be seen and heard by only one, namely God Himself. What was intended to be private communication with the Lord should be practiced in an inner room, away from the eyes and ears of all but God.

The word which the New American Standard Bible translates as "inner room" is taken from the Greek ταμεῖόν (tameion). A tameion was the innermost room in a house in Israel during the time that Jesus walked the Earth in the first century. It acted as a storeroom for grain, which is consistent in how this same Greek word is translated in Luke 12:24. It was also a windowless room which could also be considered a first-century equivalent of a modern-day "panic room" for protection from hostile intruders.

There is an interesting irony in the Lord Jesus' pointing to the use of the innermost room of a house as a place for prayer. The innermost room of the House of God, the Jerusalem Temple, was the Holy of Holies. Access was granted to that room only once a year, on the Day of Atonement, and to only one man, the High Priest (see Leviticus 16). As I mentioned above, the inner room of a typical house in Israel of that time would act as a storeroom. It was the equivalent of a food pantry in homes today. Yet, a room intended for everyday use could serve as a type of "Holy of Holies" which would allow anyone in the house to have access to God. Such is the confidence we are granted by God to enter that inner room to meet with Christ.

There are modern equivalents to the "inner room" of the first century that can serve as a type of "Holy of Holies" for you. Perhaps it is a nearby park. It might be an empty conference room at work or an empty classroom at school. Perhaps, it is inside our cars as we drive. The 20th century pastor and author A.W. Tozer, in his early years in the faith, cleared out a corner of the basement of his family's house in Akron, Ohio as a place to meet with Christ.5 In fulfilling the Lord Jesus' call and pattern to have times of prayer away from the eyes and ears of others, you must seek your own contemporary inner room to commune with the Lord.

The Value of Solitude

The Command Module (i.e., Capsule) example offers you a pattern to follow. It recognizes the value of solitude. As you will see, the value of that time away will benefit more than you. By adopting this pattern, you will learn to isolate yourself for the purpose of growing in your life in Christ.

Such times of solitude can provide you with opportunities for prayer, the reading of Scripture, reflection, and a variety of other activities. It can be the opportunity to simply think through who God is calling you to be. Perhaps, it may be a time of prayer for the wisdom to know what you are being called to do during this season of your life. However, the times of connection to re-enter your community must come along with those times of solitude. That is when you need to relate to those around you and to live the life God is calling you to live alongside them.

Such an ongoing cycle of solitude and connection has biblical precedent. In the Gospel accounts of the life of Christ, we find that He took time to isolate Himself for prayer (Matthew 14:23; Mark 1:35). He also took the time to "re-immerse" with others to teach and minister to the crowds. As you will see in Chapter 9, an ongoing practice of times of solitude will have what might seem to be a paradoxical effect. It will be of benefit to you. It will also be of benefit to others. When you are refreshed in spirit, body, and mind through times of solitude, you are far better prepared to be of help to family, friends, and the community in which you live.

In the course of reading this book, you will find that the Capsule is not a physical object or place. This book is not new devotional content along the lines of such classics as *Our Daily Bread* or Spurgeon's *Morning and Evening*. Rather, the Capsule is a devotional approach. It is a mindset for finding ways to grow deeper in Christ in times of solitude with Him. This aligns with an observation by writer Richard Foster, "Solitude is more a state of mind and heart than it is a place."[6]

The suggestions you find listed here could be practiced in a solitude which includes physical isolation from others. However, solitude is not simply a matter of physical isolation. It is possible to have a mindset of solitude even while surrounded by others.

The Capsule approach is divided into six modes. These modes are: (1) The Presence Chamber, (2) The Chapter House, (3) Analog/Digital (4) Reading (5) Outdoors (6) Remembrance. Each mode will be explained and discussed in its own chapter. Each finds a foundation in Scripture.

Ultimately, my desire is that your devotional life will be *"transformed by the renewing of your mind"* (Romans 12:2). However, before embarking on an exploration of these modes, I need to supply a "field guide" for how you can best access the Capsule, which is the topic of Chapter 1.

Chapter 1

Before Entering the Capsule

To better understand and apply the ideas being presented here, it will be helpful if you are introduced to some ideas about how to best use this book; they have been summarized into three main points.

Remember, the Capsule is a mindset for Christian devotional practice. It is a devotional approach. It is not additional devotional content. It is meant to help you develop a mindset for approaching the content you already use. This book is intended to help you answer the questions of how to use your devotional material and why you use the content you've chosen.

The Lord Jesus instructs *"But when you pray, go into your room and shut the door and pray to your Father who is in secret"* (Matthew 6:6). Note that His instruction does not supply any devotional content. Rather, He supplies you with an approach. The importance of this command is to pray in solitude. History bears out that while the content of your prayers is important, the heart and mind with which they are approached are important as well.

Second, please read this book as a collection of suggestions and recommendations. The end of each chapter will have several takeaways and suggestions. These are meant to not only supply you with a brief summary of the chapter's contents, but are also designed to help encourage you to be creative in developing your own devotional approaches.

The Capsule

These are suggestions, not commandments. I want to intentionally avoid presenting these ideas in a "you must do this" manner. While I believe that what I present here is useful and *compatible* with the Bible, it is not *commanded* in the Bible. Unfortunately, there are times when even a well-intended believer in Christ will tell a fellow believer "You must do this" regarding practices which the Bible never commands. Those who are teachers of the things of Christ must be very careful to not bind one's conscience to something which God in Christ never commanded. That is simply another way of saying that good ideas thought up by the best-intended humans cannot be made of equal authority with God's words found in the Bible.

Third, while I believe that these modes/mindsets provide you with useful boundaries, there will be some overlap of ideas within these modes. For example, the chapters on the Presence Chamber and on reading and using an analog or digital approach overlap when it comes to your intake of Scripture. In times of solitude, should you read the Bible in print or digitally? That is only one example.

Practicing the Capsule

Throughout this book, you will see references to "Capsule practice" or for you to be "practicing the Capsule "; you might wonder what this means. This simply has to do with your way of adapting these modes to your devotional life.

Your time and circumstances might allow you to practice all six modes of the Capsule in the morning before you otherwise start your day. These could possibly be spread out through the day, or even a week, month, or a year. Some practices don't easily allow for simply checking off the boxes on a "things to do" list. The mode of remembrance, for example, is something that could be practiced daily (by seeing something you purposely set up as a visual reminder). Your practice of remembrance might be spread out to a monthly review of your own notes on your life. It might involve a special memory brought back to mind annually, such as Thanksgiving, Christmas, or a birthday. Perhaps it would involve practicing these not only daily but weekly, monthly, and yearly as well.

The intent of Capsule practice is to give you tools to use to supply some added structure to your devotional life. Take these as suggestions, not commands. Please don't let practicing the Capsule become a spiritually legalistic burden. These modes are meant to assist what you're already doing. They might be helpful if you are looking to start or expand your devotional life. Use them as they serve you well. They are not an end in themselves.

Lastly, I offer you these ideas about a devotional approach because I have personally found them helpful. My hope is that you will also find them helpful. This set of ideas is hardly exhaustive. In reading this book, you might develop some approaches of your own. I encourage that. Be creative.

Takeaways:
1. The Capsule is a devotional mindset and approach; it is not devotional content.
2. This book is intended to give you some helpful suggestions. They are points of advice; They are not additional "you must do this" commands.
3. Be willing to think in creative ways about how you can approach times of solitude with God in Christ.

Chapter 2

Presence Chamber

"My Presence will go with you, and I will give you rest."
Exodus 33:14

A feature of many English castles over the last thousand years was a room known as the Presence Chamber. This room was specifically designed for a king or queen to meet with court officials and foreign dignitaries as well as commoners. The monarch sat on a throne within this chamber. In addition, the Presence Chamber allowed for royal business to be conducted with the parties involved being all in one place.

The very name of the room reminds those who are interacting with the king or queen that they are in the very presence of a monarch. Keeping this in mind would influence their speech and their behavior. It makes a difference how you think and act when you know that you are looking your monarch in the face.

The people of God have a history of encountering God, their true and eternal King, in what could also be called a Presence Chamber as well. Shortly after the Israelites left Egypt under the leadership of Moses

> *Whenever Moses entered the tent, the pillar of cloud would descend and stand at the entrance of the tent; and the LORD would speak with Moses. When all the people saw the pillar of cloud standing at the entrance of the tent, all the people would arise and*

> *worship, each at the entrance of his tent. (Exodus 33:7-8)*

The Holy of Holies, in both its tent form under Moses and the first permanent Temple built by Solomon, was like a Presence Chamber. The Ark of the Covenant, the throne of God on Earth, was situated in the Holy of Holies. The encounters with God in that Presence Chamber were limited to the High Priest (a descendant of Aaron, Moses' brother), once a year during the Day of Atonement ceremony (See Leviticus 16).

That earthly Presence Chamber was based on a pattern of heavenly things (See Hebrews 8:5). There is also a Heavenly Presence Chamber. It is good to remember that in the Heavenly Presence Chamber, the Lord Jesus is already there, sitting at the right hand of the throne of God, praying for His people (Hebrews 2).

The imagery of the Presence Chamber is not new. It found a place in the writings of the 17th century English Puritans. Thomas Watson (1620-1686) wrote, "A humble heart glories in this, that it is the presence chamber of the great and glorious King!"[7] His contemporary, Thomas Brooks (1608-1680), wrote, "The soul of Mary Magdalene was full of devils; and yet Christ cast them out, and made her heart his house, his presence chamber."[8] Clearly, these writers understood the usefulness of comparing the place of meeting an earthly monarch with the place where you meet our heavenly monarch.

One of God's attributes is His Omnipresence. This means that God is at all times and everywhere present. As a result, no place in all of creation can be a truly God-forsaken place.

This is important for us to remember. While those lone Apollo astronauts in their capsules were cut off from human communication, they never left the presence of the Lord, even on the far side of the Moon.

The same holds true for you as you approach God in the Presence Chamber of your Capsule. Again, be mindful that when you encounter God in the Presence Chamber, it is not as if He were there only and nowhere else. You never leave His presence. To speak of entering His presence is rather a recognition that you enter into a time and place in which you specially recognize His presence.

Coram Deo

Believers in Christ are called to live the entirety of life "Coram Deo" (Latin for "In the presence of God"). As theologian R.C. Sproul noted, "To live Coram Deo is to live one's entire life in the presence of God, under the authority of God, to the glory of God." 9 Living your entire life in God's presence does not lessen the value of the time you spend recognizing and remembering God's presence in a special way when you are in church. Why not also when you encounter God in the solitude of the Presence Chamber?

In more contemporary terms, a Presence Chamber allowed a monarch to interact with his subjects. The Presence Chamber is a place of encounter. As you enter, go with the knowledge that as a believer in Christ, you are being invited in. You are called to approach God's throne of grace boldly (Hebrews 4:16) since He wants that time with you.

The Presence Chamber approach reminds us to encounter Christ as the supreme, yet approachable king. He is willing to hear you and be with you. For centuries, Christians have understood that the prime ways of doing this have been through the intake of Scripture, reflection on that Scripture, and prayer.

Here are two suggestions about how you may wish to approach a time of solitude in the Presence Chamber with the Lord.

First, keep something with you during that time that will remind you that you are in the Lord's Presence. During the time of their forty-year wandering in the wilderness, the Lord commanded the Israelites to place a cord of blue on the tassels of their garments. Why?

> *... it shall be a tassel for you to look at and remember all the commandments of the Lord, to do them, not to follow after your own heart and your own eyes, which you are inclined to whore after. So you shall remember and do all my commandments, and be holy to your God. (Numbers 15:39-40)*

To remember the Lord should cause you to remember that you live in His presence.

Be mindful that you never leave God's Presence. Remember to have your own version of the blue tassel. You are seeking to remember His Presence in a special way. Eastern Orthodox believers light a candle as they enter church to remind them of Christ who is *"the light of the world"* (John 9:5). Perhaps, adopting this pattern of lighting a candle could provide you the imagery and reminder which it has provided for followers of Christ over the centuries.

A lit candle could also serve to remind you of Christ's presence as mentioned in the book of Revelation. In the second chapter, we encounter a Christ who walks among the seven candlesticks (see Revelation 2:1 in the King James Version). You may find some other practice to be beneficial. As I counsel throughout this book, be creative.

Second, you may wish to use a timer while in the Presence Chamber. The amount of time you can devote to this, as well as when you do this during the day might possibly vary, based on your schedule and the current circumstances of your life. One benefit of using a timer (with some type of audible or visual alarm) will indicate when your time has ended. It can free you from the distraction of continually looking at a clock or a watch. Not only will a timer give you a good sense of managing your time in the Capsule but also allows you to focus, not on the clock, but on encountering God in Christ.

I will not recommend a specific time of day. That will vary based on your current level of commitments (such as family, job, etc.). I highly recommend that whatever time you choose, intentionally set this time aside as a priority. It can be too easy to "trade down" and accept the priorities of others as our priorities. We find a warning about this in the Lord Jesus' parable of the Sower. The seed of the Word of God can be choked out by thorns, which represent *"the cares and riches and pleasures of life"* (Luke 8:14). It is sobering to understand that the cares of this world, as legitimate as they are, can rob you of the attention you need to pay to God if they, not God, become your focus. You will have earthly concerns. However, it is a matter of discernment to recognize when those concerns, rather than God, become the focus of your attention.

The Capsule

In revisiting the theme of the lone Apollo astronaut in orbit behind the Moon, I would like you to reflect on what it meant for those lone astronauts to be behind the Moon. They were cut off, for a time, from communication with all other humans. Think through what this would be like for one who lives in the 21st century. For a period of time, there would be no radio, no television, no internet, no cell phone communication. Would you see this "behind the Moon" time as an opportunity or a misfortune?

When you think about it, you will see that those Apollo capsules served as the ultimate inner room. Those capsules provided a time and place fully apart from all of humanity. Yet, in that isolation arose the opportunity to meet with the King of Creation, undistracted by others. While it is likely you will never visit the back side of the Moon, you too can, for a short time, isolate yourself to meet with the King of Creation in His Presence Chamber.

Takeaways:
1. The concept of a Presence Chamber, where you encounter and interact with the Divine Monarch, God Himself, can serve you well in how you look to encounter God in Christ.
2. Some possible ways of encountering God can be found by reading Scripture, reflecting on Scripture, and prayer.
3. Consider your time with God as an intentional priority. Others might distract you from a godly focus, even with such noble-sounding things as worry and concern.
4. Be creative in how you view and apply the Presence Chamber mode of the Capsule. Ask yourself what

might distract you during these times and what you can do to lay those distractions aside.

Chapter 3

Chapter House

"Look carefully then how you walk, not as unwise but as wise, making the best use of the time, because the days are evil."
Ephesians 5:15-16

A prominent feature of the monastic abbeys of Europe throughout medieval times was the Chapter House. Due to its importance, it was typically the second-largest area of an abbey other than the church itself. In England, the Chapter House of Westminster Abbey in London was so large that it not only served the needs of the Benedictine monks who lived there but was also, for a time, used as the gathering place for Parliament.

The Chapter House served primarily as the place where the resident monks would gather, typically after the services of the Divine Office of Prime (6am) or Terce (9am). This is where the business of the monastery was conducted. While "holding chapter" the monks performed a number of tasks.

One of those tasks was listening to a reading of a chapter from the text of the rule of that monastic order; the rule meaning a collection of regulations for conducting monastic life. It is where the name of this part of the building came from. For example, prior to the English monasteries being dissolved by King Henry VIII in the late 1530s, the Benedictine monks who lived at Westminster Abbey would hear one chapter read every morning from the rule of their founder, Benedict of Nursia (480-547 AD).

The Capsule

Another of those tasks in which the monks would engage, morning by morning, was a rather practical one. It centered on the discussion of the day-to-day business of the abbey and the distribution of work assignments for the monks. A phrase associated with the Benedictine Order is "Ora et Labora" (Latin for "Pray and Work"). Prayer was conducted in the church. The work of the monks started in the Chapter House.

The Chapter House was conducted in community. However, the Capsule approach discussed in this book is geared for use by an individual in solitude. While this should be done with the aim of being of service to the community as a result of your time of solitude, your practice of "holding chapter" would be between God and yourself.

There are practices that can be adapted from what those monks did every morning in the Chapter House and applied to your contemporary life in Christ. Not every practice of those early Chapter Houses can or should be brought to today. For your purposes, two of those practices will be examined to see how they can be applied here and now.

A Rule of Life

One practice that can be brought forward to today is using a rule of life. A rule of life is intended to supply structure to your life as a follower of Christ. Such rules have been used throughout church history, on both the group and the individual level. A rule of life can be of great benefit.

I have stressed in this book that the recommendations given here are simply that. Recommendations. There is nothing stated in Scripture, either explicitly or hinted at, that you must construct a personal rule of life. It can be very helpful but it is not mandatory.

I think that everyone already has a rule of life. However, the underlying question is "how did it get there?" Consider your priorities in life. Have they been purposely and intentionally thought through? Are they simply the result of your default decisions in day-to-day life?

A rule of life can allow you to think through and then act on what is truly important to you in your season of life. Your available time to act on these important things will vary with the demands placed on you in those seasons of life. The years just after high school will look different from later times which may involve further education, marriage, and child-raising. The years building and maintaining a career will look different from time spent in retirement.

In the midst of your idealism, be realistic as well. In your desire to commit to acting on your priorities, show yourself grace as well. For example, parents who are raising two children under the age of two might have the simple goal of ensuring that they pray the Lord's Prayer once a day. A retiree may wish to use his now larger amount of available time in service to others, hours which were not available during his working days. The goal of reading that large book you've always wanted to complete will be easier if you allow yourself to be satisfied that, on some busy days, reading only one page per day will still allow you to eventually complete the book.10

However, there is one particular pitfall to be avoided. This can happen when an individual takes a rule of life and turns it into their own personal law. You might, unwittingly, try to follow your rule as if it carried the authority of a biblical command. If that happens, a dangerous shift in your thinking would have occurred. Your practice would have morphed from being a useful practice to a self-imposed mandatory practice. Consider the needless guilt you might heap upon yourself for missing a day of a voluntary practice. A good and helpful practice would devolve into a legalistic, self-inflicted burden.

The practice of an early morning, daily "quiet time" provides an example of where a good idea can (without the proper caution) turn into something it was never intended to be. A Quiet Time practice involves a time of prayer, Scripture reading and reflection. All of these are, of course, good things. Daily prayer is implicitly commanded by the Lord. The request of "Give us this day our daily bread" found in Matthew 6:11, indicates praying to God for bread on a daily basis. A pattern for ongoing, continual meditation on Scripture can be found in Psalm 1:2 and Joshua 1:8.

However, there is no command given us in the Bible to read the Bible daily, whether in the early morning or any other time of the day. This is important to keep in mind concerning much of the contemporary thinking around Quiet Time practice. Unfortunately, a lot of the current literature on Quiet Time (QT) leaves the impression that it isn't optional. The authors of this literature, as well-intended as they may be, fail to take history into account. It is only at a time in history when Bibles are easily affordable, available (either in print or digitally), and translated into a language you can read that QT could be begin to be adopted as a large-scale devotional practice. This practice, as it is known today, has only been present in western nations since the middle of the 20th century, with roots only a century earlier than that. 11 These factors make the case that the overwhelming majority of believers throughout church history could never have practiced QT as it is known today. How could a practice, regarded by many today as mandatory for Christians, be required when so few believers in history (and even today around the world) could participate?

Kevin DeYoung summarizes what I believe is a good approach to what could constitute the core of the role of a daily quiet time in one's rule of life:

> I am not anti-quiet time or anti-daily devotions or anti-family worship. All of these disciplines serve God's people well and have been around for a long time. What does not serve God's people well is the unstated (and sometimes stated) assumption—put upon us by others or by ourselves—that Christianity is only for super-disciplined neatniks who get up before dawn, redeem every minute of the day, and have very organized sock drawers. Spiritual disciplines are great (and necessary) when the goal is to know God better. Spiritual disciplines are soul-crushing when the aim is to get our metaphysical workout in each day, knowing that we could always exercise more if we were better Christians.[12]

Keeping this in mind, I suggest centering a rule of life on one, two, or at most three areas where you need to grow in Christ. Constructing a rule using a large number of items could lead to a scattered focus. If that happens, many items might end up each getting a little attention with no real growth in any one of them. Keep it simple and focused.

The Capsule

Pray to the Lord for wisdom to know the areas in which you really need to grow in this time of your life. The following are some possible areas around which to build a rule of life:

1. Reading the entirety of the Bible
2. Prolonged study of one section of Scripture
3. Building up your prayer life by spending more time or focus on those needing prayer
4. Working in an area of service to others
5. Committing to being kind and Christ-like to difficult individuals

This is not an exhaustive list. If you took the time, you could likely come up with ten, twenty, thirty or more areas. I highly recommend finding those one to three items which need your commitment and God's grace in this season of your life.

Please remember that the good practices of those you know in the faith can help you construct your rule of life. The Apostle Paul wrote to the church in Corinth: "*Be imitators of me, as I am of Christ*" (1 Corinthians 11:1). Who are those you know or have known who you could imitate as they imitated and patterned Christ? Perhaps, you overheard your mother's daily prayers as she prayed for you and all your siblings by name. You may have been on the receiving end of a fellow believer's hospitality with a prepared meal while you were going through a health crisis. Of course, these examples could be added to by the hundreds. As you think through these patterns of Christ-likeness, ask yourself if there is something in those examples that you would like to pattern for your rule of life. It may be forming a rule to pray each night for your children or grandchildren by name. Perhaps, it is forming a rule to bring a meal to someone in your circles of influence who is undergoing a health crisis. Be creative.

Please remember that a rule of life is intended to help you. It should serve you. You must not serve it. A lesson from Scripture aids in describing our mindset to the value of a rule of life. In the Gospel of Mark, chapter 2, verses 23 to 28, an account is provided of the Pharisees accusing Christ's disciples of doing what is unlawful on the Sabbath. The Lord points out to them (and us) that the disciples were not in violation of the Sabbath. Rather, they were in violation of a set of man-made rules to which the Pharisees gave the authority of Scripture. The Lord Jesus made clear His point: *"The Sabbath was made for man, not man for the Sabbath"* (Mark 2:27). I believe that the same principle applies for you in how to approach constructing and living out a rule of life. A rule of life is made for a believer in Christ, not believers for a rule of life.

The Purposeful Need to Redeem the Time

The second part of how you can "hold chapter" has to do with the practical, day-to-day planning of what the Lord has called you to do. Ephesians 5:16 indicates that all believers in Christ are commanded in Scripture to make the best use of their time. We're also reminded that, for those in Christ, there are works which have been assigned to you by God from the foundation of the world. (Ephesians 2:10).

I suspect there are times when an artificial barrier is set up between what is called spiritual and what is called practical. Yet, all of life is called to be lived in the presence of God. For a believer in Christ, all of life is spiritual and is also practical. Purposely planning the activities of one's day must never be separated from the command that even in the smallest of things, you are to give glory to God (1 Corinthians 10:31).

How do you do that? There is no one specific time-organizing method or product that I am promoting here. My purpose in this chapter is to call you to intentionally plan out your assigned tasks, not necessarily how you should do that.

Handwritten calendar? Electronic calendar? (As you will see, this overlaps with the mode of analog/digital practice discussed in the next chapter). I recommend that you adopt methods that are suited to your temperament and season of life. Those methods might be handwritten, digital or a mixture of both. Once again, be creative in the methods you use.

Here is how I handle my things to do list. You might find this beneficial. My list has two categories – one includes the items that can simply be checked off as completed or not. The other category falls under the "Attitudinal" items. These things require a change in mindset to complete them. It may be helpful to adopt the approach which Jonathan Edwards (1703-1758) followed for his resolutions. He did a weekly review to see how he was doing.13 Perhaps, a similar approach will help you, especially in the Attitudinal category.

In recent years, my main "attitudinal" thing to do has been to "look for the burning bush." This approach entered my thinking a number of years ago after I was introduced to a poem called "Aurora Leigh." It was written by the American poet Elizabeth Barrett Browning and published in 1856. Within this epic poem, there is a reference to the burning bush which Moses encountered in the wilderness of Sinai (see Exodus 3:2). It was a strange sight; a bush on fire yet not burning up. Moses took the time to observe and then recognize how strange this was.

In the poem, Browning wrote:

Earth's crammed with heaven,
And every common bush afire with God;
But only he who sees, takes off his shoes,
The rest sit round it and pluck blackberries,
And daub their natural faces unaware
More and more from the first similitude.[14]

This is a reminder to me that God is still at work in our world. I want to be one who looks purposefully, to see the hand of the Lord in our times and circumstances. This type of task can't be checked off a list. My time in the Chapter House serves to remind me of that on a daily basis.

The importance of the Chapter House is its goal for intentionality in the use of time. Your focus in life can drift without purposeful effort. Your own, personally crafted rule of life serves to remind you of what is uniquely important in your life in Christ at this season of life.

Mission-Critical Instructions

During all phases of their missions, the Apollo astronauts had numerous checklists to follow to ensure the success of their missions. It has been observed that these checklists were an important part of the equipment assigned to the spacecraft, and enabled the astronauts to perform their tasks in a consistent and orderly way, while at the same time ensuring that no steps were missed or overlooked.[15]

These checklists played a very important role in the flight of Apollo 11. Of that flight, it has been said that checklists proliferated to every corner of the habitable environment of

Apollo 11; so much so that they became what astronaut Michael Collins called the spacecraft's "fourth crew member" and, for all intents and purposes, its real commander.16

In a similar way, your personally crafted rule of life can act as a checklist for the mission to which God calls you. A rule of life can provide you structure. It acts as a systematic reminder as you spend time in the Capsule. It can keep you focused on what you understand to be of most importance to you at this season in your life.

Takeaways:
1. Using the concept of a Chapter House can help you to organize the good works which God calls you to do.
2. Developing a personal rule of life can give structure to the practice of your life and reflect your spiritual priorities. It can help prevent you from falling into a default mode of life which is dominated by your unconscious habits and the agendas of others.
3. Examine different life-organizing methods to see which will work best for you.
4. It is important to be intentional in making the best use of the time that God has given you.

Chapter 4

Analog/Digital

"Therefore every scribe who has been trained for the kingdom of heaven is like a master of a house, who brings out of his treasure what is new and what is old." Matthew 13:52

At Christmas time, several years ago, I became aware of a new trend. It was the resurgence of the sale of vinyl records. As I did my Christmas shopping, I was surprised to see the amount of vinyl records being sold alongside other media such as compact discs. The electronics department of one store that I visited featured a sale on portable record players. This felt like a little trip back in time for me; a newly manufactured record player was something that I hadn't seen in stores for several decades.

I was also surprised to learn that these had become very popular with a younger generation, born when vinyl records and record players were seemingly becoming a part of the past. I asked a member of my weekly Bible study if her daughters, ranging in age from the late teens to the early twenties, were a part of this trend. She said they were.

In searching this trend on the Internet, I found that the Victrola company, a name which was synonymous with record players decades ago, was once again producing record players. One product of theirs which I found particularly intriguing was their "eight-in-one" player. It plays vinyl records, compact discs, cassette tapes, FM radio, accepts Bluetooth and auxiliary input and plays mp3 files from a flash drive. I happened to mention this to my wife during a conversation. Apparently, I gave her enough information about it as she surprised me with an "eight-in-one" as a birthday gift several months later.

I keep this in my office at home and use it almost daily. Its wooden exterior reminds me of old radio sets which I saw in my grandparents' houses when I was a boy. The look and feel of those classic devices of the early 20th century can be found in the "eight-in-one." However, several features on the unit, such as a small liquid-crystal display and compact disc player, clearly belong to the early 21st century. While using this device, it occurred to me that this player contains the best features of analog and digital. I believe that this "best of both worlds" approach toward analog and digital can be beneficial to us today in our devotional lives.

It wasn't until the closing years of the 20th century that a meaningful discussion about the comparative benefits of analog and digital approaches to Christian devotion and practice could begin. This chapter will explore devotional practices that can be done in either analog or digital mode, keeping in mind the need to seek the wisdom to know which is better for you to use in a particular time and place. It is presented at this point in the book to provide a foundation for the forthcoming chapter on reading.

Defining Our Terms

The analog/digital divide can be a little tricky to define. I think it's something that is more easily recognized than defined. For that reason, I am providing examples in place of a lengthy definition.

Analog devices rely on providing information based on some type of comparison. Consider an old-fashioned, analog clock. The one with the large and small hands. The position of those hands, in relation to the numbers on the faceplate, shows us how much time has passed for those large and small hands to get where they are now. With such a clock, you tell time based on a comparison.

Many devices of earlier eras relied on this kind of comparison approach. Thermometers offer a further example. Whether they are constructed to have a pointer sweep over a dial or to measure the expansion of a column of mercury next to a temperature scale, you can see that analog was the method for measurement.

Compare this to their digital counterparts. A digital clock and a digital thermometer each supply a display based simply on the use of digits. No comparison. Just numbers. For our purposes, our definition will be a rather simple one. Analog is not digital.

Keep this in mind as the discussion unfolds concerning the use of analog and digital in your Capsule devotional time. As the 21st century began, there were numerous predictions of how digital would replace analog in areas such as recorded music, books, and photography. However, as the 21st century unfolds, analog is reasserting itself. It has found a place in areas where its death was thought certain only a few years earlier.

The comments at the start of this chapter offer clear evidence. Vinyl LP (Long Playing) records and record turntables are making a comeback. Print books were once thought to be on the verge of extinction with the rise of e-books and e-book readers such as Kindle or Nook. Yet, print books have consistently outsold their digital counterparts over the last decade prior to this writing. What may seem counter-intuitive to an older generation are the findings about how younger generations interact with print books. Many of them live lives of continual connection through a smartphone yet prefer to read books in physical print format. [17]

These trends demonstrate that we live in a world in which analog and digital can and do co-exist. Our exploration of analog and digital in how you conduct your devotional life takes this approach. There is a place for analog. There is a place for digital. You live in an era in which you have the best of both worlds. Therefore, my recommendations won't take the form of analog versus digital. They will take the form of exploring which works better for what you are looking to do.

The purpose of this chapter is to explore questions about your use of analog or digital practices as you invest your time of solitude with Christ in the Capsule. Pray for wisdom. Discover and weigh your options. There is wisdom in exploring which mode works better for you. Be willing to reconsider your immediate preferences to recognize the possible benefits of a different approach.

A Matter of Timing

Analog excels when things can be taken more slowly while digital is better-suited when something must be done more quickly. As an example, let's apply this to journaling. For many years, I used journaling software to record my diary entries for the day. Having become a reasonably good typist, I could type out a journal entry rather quickly. It has only been in the last decade that I've switched to writing my journal entries longhand on paper with ink. In this season of my life, I want to be more reflective in my journal entries. A digital approach served me well in the past. An analog approach serves me well today. As an empty-nester, I have more time to write out a journal in long-hand rather than typing. For myself at this season of my life, historian David McCullough's observation proves itself true: "Writing is thinking. To write well is to think clearly."18

Speed and efficiency are deeply ingrained into our culture's thinking. We might take for granted that doing something quickly must be better than doing that same thing slowly. In response to this, there is a growing recognition that faster is not always better. This shift in thinking has contributed to the growth of the Slow Reading and Slower Living movements. These movements have evolved from the desire by many to take life at a more leisurely pace.

Perhaps due to the cultural "air that we breathe", it may never have occurred to you that some practices that you do in the Capsule can be done more slowly. Bible reading is an important example. You may have a mindset of making sure that you get through your day's reading, especially if you're on a plan that takes you through the entire Bible in one year. Without intending it, your goal may have shifted from taking in God's Word to that of simply completing the reading.

This takes wisdom while factoring in your current life circumstances. Perhaps your obligations at this time in your life allow you only a handful of minutes for prayer and the Word. However, perhaps you haven't considered that you may have more time for Capsule activities than you've realized. In other words, take this as permission to live your life in Christ a bit more slowly.

Ease of Use

Consider well which technologies to use when in the Capsule. (I consider a pen and paper as technology, low-level by 21st century standards yet still a technology). Ask yourself how easy it is for you to use that technology for your intended purpose. Let's use the example of taking notes. In this example, you're walking in a forest, spending time in prayer, and reflecting on the wonders of God's creation. During that time, you think of something you want to remember for later. How do you create and retain that note?

Perhaps you have a smartphone with you. You might find it easy to type notes into a Notes app or use a speech-to-text function for a quick entry of your thoughts onto a digital note. Perhaps you're more comfortable with using a small, easy-to-carry paper notebook and pen. Both modes equally serve the purpose of recording a note and your preferences will guide which mode works better for you.

Ease of use might prompt you to switch your approach depending on your needs at the time. I toggle between using a paper Bible and a Bible app on a Kindle for my personal devotional reading. However, when I am teaching a Tuesday night Bible study, I use a Bible app on my laptop. It helps with readability and the need to quickly navigate from one passage to another or even one translation to another. Using a print copy of the Bible would take far more time in that circumstance. As I stress throughout this book, be flexible.

Keep in mind that switching approaches can be prompted by a change in capabilities. In other words, a change in your immediate circumstances might not allow you to use your technology of choice. Knowing about other technologies can provide helpful alternatives. My own life circumstances during the writing of this book serve as an example. I had open-heart surgery while I was writing the book. A side effect of the surgical procedure, due to how I was placed on the operating table, caused the ulnar nerve in my right hand to be compressed. My ring and pinky fingers were numb as a result. For a right-handed person like me, handwriting and even typing were impossible for several weeks after surgery.

It was during that time that I learned to use the Notes app on my smartphone, with its speech-to-text capability for things I'd normally write out on paper. Fortunately, the nerve compression did resolve itself. I'm back to writing and typing as well as occasionally using speech-to-text. I'm so grateful that, for my season of recovery, a technological note-taking alternative was available to me.

When considering which technology to use, make wise choices based on your preferences and abilities. In a digital age, many still prefer the look and feel of a physical, print book. However, many in the older generations prefer to use a digital device for their Bible reading because the font size can be increased or decreased for better visibility. (Clearly, something you cannot do with a print Bible.)

Accessibility

While delivering the eulogy at the funeral of R.C. Sproul in December of 2017, John MacArthur observed that the world is living through the time of the greatest explosion of truth in history.[19] He went on to list the capabilities available to people around the world, such as accessing the Internet with relatively inexpensive digital devices. This has allowed millions to hear the truth of God's Word in ways which were unimagined even a generation ago.

Consider what is now available to you. Sermons, lectures, podcasts, audio, and video recordings are only a part of what is now accessible, typically through a free download. Many smartphone Bible apps can bring up not only a wide variety of translations of Scripture but also provide an audio of the section of Scripture which you're reading.

It's not as if these things were not available through analog means in years past. Charles Haddon Spurgeon's sermons were printed, in their entirety, in London newspapers in the late 1800s. In the 20th century, there were recordings of the Bible on vinyl records. Many of the sermons delivered by A. W. Tozer in the 1950s and 1960s were recorded with the technology of that time.

There are two aspects of accessibility that will be explored here. Specifically, those of speed and volume. In the early Internet era, only a generation or two ago, it may have taken several weeks to receive a printed book ordered online, but now it can be received in a day.

Sermon videos and audios are now so common, from so many churches, that you can access those sermons, in full, later in the day (speed). You can now search for sermons and teaching content from other churches as well (volume). The digital world has opened an extremely abundant treasure trove of resources which can be accessed quickly. I suggest that you familiarize yourself with digital-device apps and content providers who supply the fuel for what MacArthur referred to as an "explosion of truth." For further resources, please see the Resources tab on my website, Restoring the Core.

Hybrid Approach

Lastly, I'd like to suggest that there are occasions for what I call a hybrid approach. It merges aspects of both the analog and digital approaches. Once again, let me use a real-life example. Several years ago, I found out about a book which then nine-year old George Washington received in 1741. It remained in his library for the rest of his life.

The book's title, *The Sufficiency of a Standing Revelation,* intrigued me. I thought it may have been a defense of the sufficiency of an unchanging Scripture over time. As it turned out, it was. The book contains eight lectures which make the case that Scripture is timeless and sufficient for each and every generation. As an aside, it is a remarkable book. I highly recommend it. You might struggle at first with the 18th century font in which the letter "s" looks like a letter "f." Overcoming this small hurdle is worth the investment of effort to gather up the "spiritual gold" you will find in that book. The URL for accessing the pdf is in the Endnotes.[20]

The version I found was a digitized copy of the original printing of 1700. That digitized version was available as a pdf. My personal preference is not to read pdfs on a tablet unless the content is only a few pages. "*Sufficiency"* was much larger than that. I downloaded the pdf, printed a hardcopy, three-hole punched it and placed it into a binder. This hybrid approach allowed me use both a digital and analog approach to reading this book.

The Capsule

Lessons from one capsule to use in your own

The Apollo astronauts of the late 1960s to early 1970s used a hybrid approach during their missions of lunar exploration. In their capsule, they used both analog and digital resources to successfully complete their missions. Their combining of those resources can serve as a pattern for us as well.

In terms of digital resources, both the Apollo Command Module and Lunar Excursion Module were equipped with a (then) state-of-the-art digital Apollo Guidance Computer (AGC). The AGC was used for navigation and control of the spacecraft. Among the analog resources used on those flights were a sextant, paper star charts, and a slide rule.

Sextants date back to the 18th century. They were used by sailors to determine their ship's position, based on sightings of the Sun, Moon or certain stars. The Apollo sextant played a similar role for those space-faring travelers. This and the paper star charts acted as a way of confirming their position in space. The slide-rule was invented in the early 17th century. It was still being used in the Apollo era as an analog computing device at the time just before the advent of handheld calculators. Slide rules were used for computations which involved multiplication and division.

The use of analog and digital on the Apollo missions shows how the two collaborate. State-of-the-art digital technology played its necessary role. Sextant technology invented in the 18th century was used alongside a digital computer as well as printed maps to contribute to the need for the Apollo astronauts to chart their position in space.

In planning how you approach the time in your Capsule, evaluate what will work best for you. There are times when you might wish to toggle between analog and digital as it will serve you well in your current circumstances. Explore both modes. A mode you may not have considered could turn out to be more beneficial than you thought.

Be creative. Be wise and thankful. Your options for means to encounter the Lord have never been greater.

Takeaways:
1. The technology of this era allows you the options of using an analog, digital, or mixed approach to your devotional time with the Lord.
2. If you are looking to develop a slower and more deliberate devotional approach, analog practices can be of great benefit.
3. A digital approach is handy when ease-of-use is a factor.
4. The phenomenal number of digital resources available to you today must be considered as a gift from God. Your accessibility to these resources, both in terms of speed and sheer volume of accessible items, has never been greater.
5. The example of the Apollo astronauts in their capsules shows us the benefit of a "best-of-both worlds" approach to using analog or digital technology and can supply a pattern for you in your time of solitude with Christ.

Chapter 5

Reading

"...have you not read what was said to you by God?"
Matthew 22:31b

Imagine living in a culture in which information that doesn't reside in your own head exists only in the heads of others you know. In this hypothetical culture, consider an event such as a famine or earthquake which happened in your community years ago. Perhaps you witnessed the event. But, if not, your knowing about it is reliant on someone else's memory. If it happened before you were born, you would either need to know someone who witnessed the event or know someone who heard an account of the event and passed it along orally, from one generation to another.

In such a world, your community's fund of collective knowledge is only as good as the memories of the people who are alive at the moment. The community would also need to develop ways of passing along information orally and accurately to the next generation to prevent distortion of those collective memories. Without such a method, knowledge that is important to the community, particularly historical knowledge, would become lost with the passage of time.

Passing along knowledge orally has been a very important part of human history. However, it does have its limitations. Orally passed-along knowledge is only as good as the way in which it is transmitted. Perhaps you're familiar with accounts of family stories which have been lost to time, i.e., prevented from getting passed along, due to things such as a sudden, untimely death or chronic memory issues.

There is also a known tendency for oral accounts to become distorted over time. The "Telephone" game provides a great example. A message is whispered from one player to the next. Part of the fun of the game is to see how different the original message is from what the last player says it is. The game is a good reminder of how information that is passed along orally can become distorted.

Early in human history, people discovered the importance of having "extra-somatic" knowledge. The term comes from the Latin and simply means "outside the body." The ability to record information on something other than a human brain is just a fancy way of describing the development of writing.

Extra-somatic (i.e., written) information must have a corresponding means by which the information can be decoded. Put rather simply, for writing to be useful, the corresponding skill of reading must be developed as well. For reading to be useful, you need to know such things as the characters used in writing (i.e., an alphabet). You would also need to know how to interpret the combinations of letters in an alphabet into words used in a language you know. For example, if you see a sign that says "ordinateur", you won't know what the sign is saying if you know English but don't know French. To an English-only reader, recognizing the letters in the word doesn't help you recognize that when those letters are combined in French, the word means "computer" in English.

Having access to written information from across the centuries is truly a treasure and blessing to each generation.

The New Testament was so cherished by the early church that an explosion of hand copying its texts occurred early in church history. Over 5,800 Greek language manuscripts of copies of the New Testament still exist today. Many of those copies are over 1,500 years old.21 Consider how many books have been sitting on shelves for years, or even centuries, awaiting a new audience to read and appreciate what they have to tell you.

A World Beyond Your Own

One of the wonderful benefits of reading is being able to tap into information that you might never have been able to come across yourself. Reading allows you to access information beyond your own experience, time, and place. It can give you a picture of what life was like for those in other times and places. Reading can give not only a sense of what life was like, but a sense of what was important to the writer and the people of that time.

One way this has developed for me is in my love of history. When I'm traveling, I usually find my way to whatever historical museum happens to be nearby. In reading the panels that go along with the displays, I've often found references to books which point back to the conditions of the time. This was true when my wife and I visited Philadelphia several years ago. One museum we visited was the Mütter Museum, an institution which houses historical artifacts related to the development of medicine.

One of the sections in the museum was dedicated to medical practices during the American Civil War. One display featured a collection of photographs from that era, compiled into a large poster. Among the photos was the cover of a book entitled *The Soldier's Pocket Book*. After getting back home, I found a digital copy on archive.org. [22]

As I read the book, it became evident that it had been distributed to newly enlisted Union Army soldiers. It was a Christian devotional book which dedicated a good amount of text to discussing the soldier's current role in life. It also discussed the very real possibility of facing death in battle. There was great comfort in how the author of this pocketbook (quite literally a book which could be carried in a pocket) reminded these soldier-readers: "Make God your friend at all times, and he will not forget you when you are in peril."[23]

The Soldier's Pocket Book is an example of finding information that I would not have encountered otherwise. I've never served in the military. I do not know, firsthand, what it is like to go into a battle that I might not survive. Not only did those Civil War soldiers, on both sides, face possible death on the battlefield, they faced other possible horrors depending on the extent of their injuries. The treatment of battlefield wounds during the American Civil War-era reflected the medical and surgical practices of the mid-19th century. Often, soldiers ended up dying from battle wounds which could be easily treated today. Depending on the severity of a battlefield injury, these soldiers could also face the nightmare of a battlefield amputation, performed without anesthetic. Interestingly, Civil War non-battlefield related deaths consistently outnumbered those due to battlefield injuries.

The Soldier's Pocket Book is a glimpse into the spiritual mindset of those facing the very-real horrors of war. As I know a bit about Civil War history, this book gave me insight into how those individuals faced life and death in troubling times.

It provided me with a perspective on battlefield bravery that I have never encountered.

Seeing With Another's Eyes

Reading can also give you insights from the thoughts, reflections, and experiences of others. These can come in a variety of genres. Biographies can give you a sense of the thoughts, experiences, and life circumstances of a given individual. Histories serve a similar role as a kind of biography which includes a nation or people group. Books on philosophy show you the ideas that great thinkers have pondered and wrestled with over the centuries. Fiction allows you to explore ideas in places and times that existed in the imagination of the author. Books on theology can show you the heart and mind of those who have explored what is known of God based on the text of the Bible and what can be logically deduced from it.

Crossing the Aisle

The phrase "crossing the aisle" refers to when a politician seeks to cooperate with members of an opposing party to work for the greater good of their constituents. This kind of approach can also be useful in reading. It's easy to simply read the perspectives of those with whom you agree, be it politically, philosophically, religiously, or in one of a hundred other different ways. It will definitely be a challenge to shift your approach to take the time to find out what those with whom you disagree think about a given set of ideas. You may pick up insights that might never have occurred to you.

This approach is helpful in avoiding what is called "naïve realism", 24 defined as a tendency toward holding two distinct mindsets in tandem. The first mindset is that you believe your view of the world around you is objective. The second mindset is believing that those who disagree with you are either uninformed, irrational, or biased. You will grow in your understanding if you have the courage to think that an ideological opponent may have some valuable insights for you to learn. This is not compromise. This doesn't require you to "switch streams" and adopt a new ideology. This approach will, however, allow you to grow in your knowledge and wisdom far more than staying in the "echo chamber" of reading only those with whom you agree.

Simply Different

Differences exist beyond ideology. A good way of describing these differences is found in a sermon that the Apostle Paul delivered to some curious residents of first-century Athens.

> *And he [God] made from one man every nation of mankind to live on all the face of the earth, having determined allotted periods and the boundaries of their dwelling place (Acts 17:26)*

These differences manifest themselves in ways such as gender, age, nationality, and culture. Read from those who are not like you. If you're a male, read the writings of a female author. If you live in the United States, read from someone who is not American. This can open up a sense of understanding that you would never experience otherwise.

A Time Machine

One benefit of reading is being able to take in the insights of those who have gone on before you in death. A book can act as a type of time machine. Through a book, insights, observations, and creative thoughts of a person from one era are not doomed to stay in the author's head and die with the author. Writing a book allows ideas to travel to the future where a reader can be informed, inspired, and impacted years or even centuries later.

One writer who impacted (and still impacts) me was the 17th century British minister Thomas Goodwin (1600-1680). Goodwin was a pastor and a prolific writer. Michael Reeves writes of Goodwin:

> Once ranked as a theologian alongside Augustine and Athanasius, even hailed as 'the greatest pulpit exegete [interpreter] of Paul that has ever lived', he should be a household name. His writings, while not easy, always pay back the reader, for in Goodwin a simply awesome theological intellect was wielded by the tender heart of a pastor.[25]

Goodwin has been a hero to me. He ministered in London during the plague of 1665. He survived the Great London Fire of 1666, although, unfortunately, half of Goodwin's large personal library was lost to the fire. On a personal note, during my first trip to London, my wife and I visited the gravesite of Thomas Goodwin at Bunhill Fields.

Though he died in 1680, Goodwin's writings (particularly his book, *The Heart of Christ*) have helped me to better understand the heart of love which Christ, while in Heaven now, has for His people today. I can almost imagine Thomas Goodwin sitting at his desk, writing with quill and ink the words which he would send into the future, words that many have read, including myself, over three and a half centuries later. What Goodwin, and other authors of the past, have done for us is so similar to what the writer of the New Testament letter to the Hebrews says about Abel. *"And through his faith, though he died, he still speaks."* (Hebrews 11:4).

Clearing Up Blind Spots

Reading the writers of the past can help you avoid blind spots in your thinking. It can be helpful for preventing (or curing) you from being a "chronological snob." Just as naïve realists have a distorted understanding of their own views and the views of their ideological opponents, a chronological snob distorts the value of works produced today as compared to those of the past. This perspective believes that something produced now must be better than something produced in the past for the simple reason it was produced now. It is the latest. Therefore, it must be the greatest.

C.S. Lewis wrote about "chronological snobbery" in an introductory essay he penned for a printing of *On the Incarnation* by the fourth-century bishop Athanasius. Lewis points out that people of every era have certain blind spots.

> "Every age has its own outlook. It is specially good at seeing certain truths and specially liable to make certain mistakes. We all, therefore, need the books that will correct the characteristic mistakes of our own period."[26]

These are things which a society often overlooks and simply aren't recognized as problems at that time. The large-scale presence of slavery in pre-Civil War America would have been a blind spot for many in the United States of the 18th and 19th centuries.

Our culture has blind spots today. The problem is that our culture is too close to the blind spots to recognize them as blind spots. You need the insights of those living in the past, who didn't have those same blind spots as you, to give you the insight you can only get from "outside" help. In this case, outside means outside your own time and place. Be wary of thinking that the "latest" is always the greatest. It might be. It might not.

Reading in the Capsule

Reading, of course, played an ongoing and pivotal role in the lunar-explorer astronauts' Apollo mission, whose approach is modeled and applied in this book. The very nature of the mission required the skill of reading. The reading of procedure lists and other documents was standard operating procedure. The Apollo missions could not have succeeded without the literacy of those astronauts.

However, there was one very special time of reading aboard an Apollo lunar mission which will be remembered as long as the history of space flight endures. It was on December 24, 1968, during humanity's first-ever manned trip to the Moon. Consider what the three men aboard the Apollo 8 capsule were facing that Christmas Eve. The challenges were of the kind that no traveler in space had ever encountered.

Would their spacecraft's service-module engine fire correctly within the next few hours to break them out of lunar orbit and send them on the correct return course back to Earth? Would their re-entry path into Earth's atmosphere be within the right parameters? The capsule, hurtling in from deep space, would need to encounter the atmosphere at just the right angle. Too thick? The capsule burns up. Too shallow? The capsule skips off the atmosphere back into space like a stone skipped on the surface of a pond. If it happened, those three astronauts would be stranded in space with no means of returning to Earth.

Because so many aspects of the flight of Apollo 8 were being done for the first time, the astronauts believed they had a 50/50 chance of returning to Earth safely. With all that as background, consider the message that the three astronauts wished to deliver to the people of Earth. Just wishing everyone a "Merry Christmas" would not do.

During their live broadcast from the capsule of Apollo 8 that night, astronauts Frank Borman, James Lovell, and William Anders took turns reading from the opening verses of the creation account as found in the first chapter of the book of Genesis. Centuries earlier, King David, in praising God, wrote:

> *When I look at your heavens, the work of your fingers, the moon and the stars, which you have set in place, what is man that you are mindful of him, and the son of man that you care for him? (Psalm 8:3-4).*

I suspect that King David would have marveled to know that the first three "sons of man" to visit the Moon would read from the Genesis creation account to the largest, live audience to ever hear a reading of Scripture.

Takeaways:
1. See writing and reading for the marvels that they are; they free us from having knowledge trapped only in your mind or the minds of others.
2. Reading allows you access to information, ideas, and insights beyond the limits of your own experience, time, and place.
3. Use reading as a way to build up your empathy for others as you read the writings of those with whom you differ ideologically, in gender, age, or culture.
4. The writings of those in the past are like a message sent to you in a time machine; they can offer insights for your present moment, often acting as means to see beyond the blind spots of your own time, culture, and place.

Chapter 6

Taking the Capsule Outdoors

"And Isaac went out to meditate in the field toward evening..."
Genesis 24:63

For centuries, theologians have held that God has revealed Himself to humans in two ways. One of those ways is through what is called special revelation. Special revelation provides highly detailed information about God. This includes both the written Word of God (the Bible) and the living Word of God (the Lord Jesus Christ Himself). (John 1:1-14). The second way is through general revelation. While not containing the detailed informational content of special revelation, general revelation tells us how God reveals Himself in nature.

General revelation provides clear evidence of the existence of creation's Creator. We learn from Psalm 19:1, *The heavens declare the glory of God.*

In Romans 1:19-20, we find:

> *For what can be known about God is plain to them, because God has shown it to them. For his invisible attributes, namely, his eternal power and divine nature, have been clearly perceived, ever since the creation of the world, in the things that have been made. So they are without excuse.*

Article 2 of the 16th century Belgic Confession states:

> We know [God] by two means: First, by the creation, preservation, and government of the universe, since that universe is before our eyes *like a beautiful book* in which all creatures, great and small, are as letters to make us ponder the invisible things of God." (Emphasis added)

Meditation

There are numerous examples in Scripture which call for you to meditate on God's Word. Joshua, the successor to Moses, was commanded concerning the book of the Law to "*meditate on it day and night, so that you may be careful to do according to all that is written in it.*" (Joshua 1:7) David, the king of Israel, wrote, "*I will meditate on your precepts and fix my eyes on your ways*" as well as "*I will lift up my hands toward your commandments, which I love, and I will meditate on your statutes.*" (Psalm 119:15,48)

There are also examples within Scripture of meditating on God's works in the natural world. The same David who wrote about meditating on God's word also wrote, "*Make me understand the way of your precepts, and I will meditate on your wondrous works.*" (Psalm 119:27). Elsewhere in the book of Psalms, Asaph wrote, "*I will ponder all your work, and meditate on your mighty deeds.*" (Psalm 77:12)

It is important to define terms to ensure accurate understanding of what you are reading. Meditation in the Bible differs from what is commonly called meditation in the early 21st century. Biblical meditation has its focus on God and can include reflecting on His Word or His works. Regarding the essence of biblical meditation, in "*A Christian on the Mount; A Treatise Concerning Meditation*", the 17th century

English minister, Thomas Watson (c.1620-1686) observed the following:

> "If it be inquired what meditation is, I answer—Meditation is the soul's retiring of itself, that by a serious and solemn thinking upon God, the heart may be raised up to heavenly affections."27

Meditation in western culture today takes a different approach which has much in common with eastern religious practice. Typically, this involves the effort to either empty the mind of thought or focus attention on one particular thing, such as one's breathing. Biblical meditation, rather, seeks to fill the mind. The practice engages in deep, focused thought on what Nathaniel Ranew defined as "...either pondering of spiritual things, for improving knowledge, and exciting practice; or by a weighing all other things whatever, for reducing them to a spiritual end and use."28

In more contemporary words, biblically based meditation is pondering on something spiritual or on something that can be applied spiritually.

It is also proper to note that the Hebrew word translated as meditate in Genesis 24:63 appears only once in the Bible. It is similar enough to the Hebrew word לָשׂוּחַ (lasuah) translated as "meditation" in Psalm 104:34, to justify the translation used in the Genesis passage. Clearly, Isaac was meditating or musing about something at the time when his bride was arriving from Mesopotamia.

The Capsule

More than the sum of our parts

The Christian understanding of who we humans are considers both natural and supernatural dimensions. You have a physical body, as is the case with all animals on Earth. You have a non-physical soul which will exist into eternity. A biblically-sound approach for taking care of yourself includes both your physical and spiritual self.

Physical-only care (i.e., diet, exercise) will treat you simply only as an advanced form of animal. Such an approach can lead to the view that your main goal in life is to forestall physical death as long as possible since complete extinction awaits afterwards. Soul-only care neglects the importance of the body in this lifetime. Such a way of thinking can lead to a view of life in which the body is seen primarily as a soul container. Its purpose ends at death and allows the soul to experience a permanent, bodiless freedom.

As you read the Bible, from Genesis to Revelation, you see the importance of both the natural and supernatural aspects of creation. This is especially true for us as human beings. Scripture does not paint the picture of physical death as the complete end of our existence. Nor does it present our destiny as eternally, disembodied spirits. Resurrection from the dead is clearly taught in the New Testament. The topic of resurrection is central to the fifteenth chapter of Paul's first letter to the Corinthian church. A careful reading of that chapter shows that our ultimate, future state has no room for existing as merely disembodied spirits. Clearly, our physical and spiritual sides co-exist and are interrelated.

If this is true for our eternal state, how much more so for life this side of eternity? Our mindset can affect our body.

Proverbs 17:22 tells us, *"A joyful heart is good medicine, but a crushed spirit dries up the bones."*

Unmanaged stress can play havoc with your body. The condition of your body can also affect you spiritually. Anxiety can remove the focus in your thinking. It makes sense that the apostle Peter instructed his first readers (and you in this time) to have a mindset of self-control for the purpose of being able to pray well (See 1 Peter 4:7).

Taking it Outdoors

In this chapter, my concern is to impress upon you the importance of taking your devotional life outdoors. It might seem strange to use, throughout this book, the imagery of a being in a space capsule, isolated and well away from others along with a call to encountering God in Christ devotionally in the outdoor, wide-open spaces. Consider though that the Capsule is a symbol. It is more of a mindset than a call to actual physical isolation. You can be in solitude in the great outdoors as much as being physically isolated in a ten-foot by ten-foot room at your home, school, or office. As you will see, adding an outdoor dimension to your devotional life can have spiritual, physical, emotional, and mental health benefits.

Examples Past and Present

The impact that being outdoors can have on one's life has been noted by a number of Christians over the centuries. Charles Spurgeon (1834-1891) once observed:

> He who forgets the humming of the bees among the heather, the cooing of the wood-pigeons in the forest, the song of birds in the woods, the rippling of rills

among the rushes, and the sighing of the wind among the pines, needs not wonder if his heart forgets to sing and his soul grows heavy. A day's breathing of fresh air upon the hills, or a few hours' ramble in the beech woods' umbrageous calm, would sweep the cobwebs out of the brain of scores of our toiling ministers who are now but half alive. A mouthful of sea air, or a stiff walk in the wind's face, would not give grace to the soul, but it would yield oxygen to the body, which is the next best....29

The people of God have a history of practicing their devotional life out-of-doors. In pre-Christian times, the people of Israel would sing from a set of songs as they made their three-times-a-year pilgrimages to Jerusalem. Jerusalem was set on a high hill. Thus, a journey to Jerusalem would be considered an ascent to the city. A set of these songs has been preserved for us as the "Songs of Ascents" found in Psalms 120 to 134.

In more recent times, the practice of prayer walking has gained quite a bit of attention in Christian circles. A current version of this practice dates back to the mid-1980s. It is a pre-planned effort that involves individuals walking through places like a city or neighborhood. The intent behind this activity is to pray during that walk for the various needs of the people in those communities. Whether spiritual, economic, or any of a hundred other needs, those participating in the prayer walk seek, for the duration of the walk, to identify with those individuals in that geographic location.

There is also an earlier form of prayer-walking which can be traced historically to about a century ago . . .

> A contemplative [prayer] walk is an invitation to slow down and spend time in the outdoors enjoying God's amazing creation. 30

Church history supplies further examples of those who incorporated "the great outdoors" into their devotional life. Two examples come from 17th century England. The first is Mary Rich, Countess of Warwick (1625-1678). Her reputation for being a godly woman, well-versed in biblical meditation, is mentioned in the forward of Nathanael Ranew's 1670 book *Solitude Improved by Divine Meditation.* He wrote of his "observation made of your exemplary and eminent practice of, and experienced sweetness felt in the breathings of your soul up this hill of holy meditation." 31 It was written that she "spent much time in contemplation in her garden" which she also viewed as a type of wilderness. Mary Rich made a good, purposeful use of an outdoor garden to aid her meditation on God and the things of God.

A second example is that of Isaac Ambrose (1604-1664). Tom Schwanda relates how, for a number of years, Ambrose would take a retreat which at times would be a month in length.32 He lived in a forest hut in the springtime. Keep in mind that Ambrose was not participating in some trendy, 17th century devotional practice. Such a practice was not common in his time. Isaac's journal entries, made during those times while in "the sweet silent Woods" (his words), show how, in the midst of forest solitude, God was doing a great work on Isaac.

While on his annual retreat in 1646, Ambrose's diary entry for May 20th states:

> I came to Weddicre [Woods], which I did upon mature resolution, every year about that pleasant Spring time (if the Lord pleased) to retire my self, and in some solitary and silent place to practice especially the secret Duties of a Christian: 33

In mid-17th century England, a secret duty was one which was privately practiced. Ambrose listed those secret duties he practiced. They included reviewing his diary, praying, fasting, reading the Scriptures, watchfulness, self-examination, meditation, and praising God.

In his journal entry for May 20, 1641, Ambrose wrote:

> "[t]his day in the Evening the Lord in his mercy poured into my soul the ravishing joy of his blessed Spirit. O how sweet was the Lord unto me? I never felt such a lovely taste of Heaven before." 34

Clearly, Isaac Ambrose's encounters with God while on retreat were special times of growth and a joyful deepening of his faith. His times of solitude in a forest enabled him to grow in Christ while pondering His written word.

While it might not be practical for you to isolate yourself for one month every year to spend time fellowshipping with God in Christ, there are lessons that you can learn from Mary Rich and Isaac Ambrose. Tending to a garden can take on a whole new level of spiritual meaning for you. Being out in nature can serve as a wonderful backdrop for prayer, taking in the Word (by reading or listening to an audio version), meditation, memorizing Scripture, and many other practices.

Looking Up

Taking your devotional life outdoors can have a number of different aspects. Perhaps it consists of a walk in a forest or a city park. It might be a stroll along a beach in which the power of the sea reminds us of passages in Scripture where we see the power of the sea reflecting the power of God (Psalm 46:2; Psalm 93:4) Those encounters with God happen when we look in front of us. Consider the additional devotional aspect of looking up into the sky on a clear night.

The stars cry out silent praise for their Creator. Psalm 19:1 reminds you

> *The heavens declare the glory of God, and the sky above proclaims his handiwork.*

The stars offer you objects for your meditation, not only as written about in Scripture but also in the book of nature. In Genesis 15:5, God used a starry night to illustrate the scope of His promise to Abraham:

> *[God] brought him outside and said, "Look toward heaven, and number the stars, if you are able to number them.... So shall your offspring be."*

Psalm 147:4 states, *"[God] determines the number of the stars; he gives to all of them their names."* In biblical terms, naming someone (or something) indicates the authority which the one who names has over the one named (Genesis 2:19; Genesis 1:28). God's naming of all the stars shows you His authority over the entire universe. It is also a reminder that as the vistas of observable science expand, so does the understanding of God's glory which goes along with it.

The Capsule

Like Abraham did so many centuries ago, you can look at those same stars and marvel at what God has placed there. For those in the Northern Hemisphere, perhaps the easiest star to locate in the night sky is Polaris, the North Star. Polaris is about 430 light years away from Earth. A light year is the distance that light travels in one year. Reflect on what that means. The starlight which left Polaris is 430 years old when it reaches Earth. To provide you with a sense of scale, imagine that a theatre patron of the early 21st century goes to see a Shakespearean play one night at the restored Globe Theatre in London. As he looks up, he sees the light of the North Star. The light reaching that patron's eyes left Polaris around the time when Shakespeare was writing and first producing the very play being seen that night.

As you marvel at the night sky and see the wonders which God has created, reflect on what this means for a follower of Christ. The promise remains that *"...those who are wise shall shine like the brightness of the sky above; and those who turn many to righteousness, like the stars forever and ever." Daniel 12:3.*

While you won't find your destiny in the stars, for those who follow Christ, the stars paint a picture of what our eternal destiny will look like.

The View from the Capsule

Consider the view of the book of nature which the Apollo astronauts enjoyed during their lunar missions. They could look out their capsule window to observe the clouds, oceans, and land masses of the distant Earth. They could take it in all with a single glance. With their knowledge of what the other planets of the solar system looked like, they understood the unique beauty of that "blue marble in space"[35] – which they called their home.

Their mission also gave them the opportunity to see the stars as no other humans on Earth could ever see with the unaided eye. Even in remote areas on Earth, well away from the light, pollution of cities, atmospheric haze, and turbulence still restricts some of the stars which could be otherwise seen. While in lunar orbit, during those times when the Apollo spacecraft was behind the Moon, blocked off from Earth and from sunlight, the view of the stars would be utterly majestic and awe-inspiring.

Several of those Apollo astronauts revealed the life-changing effect of their time on those missions. Their view of creation was deeply changed. Apollo 17 commander Eugene Cernan noted,

> "The Earth doesn't tumble through space; it moves with logic and certainty and with beauty beyond comprehension ... It's just too beautiful to have happened by accident. There has to be somebody bigger than you and me that put it all together. There's no question in my mind that there's a Creator of the universe. There's a God up there." [36]

James Irwin flew on Apollo 15 in August of 1971. While he was already a believer in Christ at the time of the mission, what he saw of God's creation while in space deepened his faith. He noted:

> "The Earth reminded us of a Christmas tree ornament hanging in the blackness of space. As we got farther and farther away, it diminished in size. Finally,

it shrank to the size of a marble, the most beautiful you can imagine...That beautiful, warm, living object looked so fragile, so delicate, that if you touched it with a finger it would crumble and fall apart ... seeing this has to change a man."37

While you might never have the occasion to fly to the Moon, you do have an Earthbound opportunity that can give you great benefit. Learn to read from and delight in the book written without words. It is what theologians have called "general revelation", namely, God's revelation of Himself in nature. Time spent in nature, reflecting on the things of God, is good for both your body and your soul. Learn to deepen your sense of awe in God's handiwork, of which you are a part. Marvel at the intricacy of a spider web. Reflect on the simple and yet profound design of a leaf.

Allow yourself to be amazed at sights of the night sky, as you observe the Moon and planets. Stand in awe of the majestic array of stars, each with its own God-given name. These will cause you to echo in your heart the words of King David, written over three-thousand years ago.

When I look at your heavens, the work of your fingers, the moon and the stars, which you have set in place, what is man that you are mindful of him, and the son of man that you care for him? ...O LORD, our Lord, how majestic is your name in all the earth. (Psalm 8:3,4,9)

Takeaways

1. Biblical meditation is a call to think deeply and reflect upon God, His Words, and His works.
2. Scripture demonstrates that we humans are creatures with interconnected physical and spiritual components. Benefits to one can be of benefit to the other.
3. Numerous voices from church history, such as Charles Spurgeon, Mary Rich, and Isaac Ambrose, have promoted the physical and spiritual benefits of having an outdoor devotional life.
4. Your devotional life can benefit from reflecting on nature in front of you (a forest, a beach, etc.) as well as nature as you look up (the Moon, planets, and stars).
5. There can be great benefit in periodically taking your devotional life outdoors.

Chapter 7

Remembrance

"You shall remember the LORD your God..."
Deuteronomy 8:18

This world has a way of trying to capture your attention. At this period in history in western culture, this is so much the case that a new term has risen up to describe it. It's called the "Attention Economy." The Free Dictionary defines Attention Economy as "The theory that the attention span of online users is a limited commodity that is subject to market forces. The economic model supposes the existence of a market place in which consumers agree to give their attention in exchange for services such as email or personalized news."38

Aware that your attention is truly something limited, those creating social media platforms design them to gain and keep as much of your limited attention as possible. While these platforms are driven by algorithms which tailor the content you see along the lines of your preferences, they still show you what the social media platform operators want you to see. By implication, if your attention is being directed to their chosen content for you, your attention is not available to be focused on something else.

Perhaps one way to think of the Attention Economy is to think of it as a Distraction Economy. Consider the possible distractions that seek your attention today. Social media is a given. Podcasts, on-demand videos, and streaming services are among the more current options. Don't forget the technology which has been around for several generations such as television, radio, movies, and recorded music. Your occasions for distraction have never been greater.

However, do we humans live distracted lives because of all these technologies or do we seek out those things because we inwardly crave distraction? Blaise Pascal had an interesting answer to that question. How could a French philosopher and theologian of the 17th century have insight into distraction before inventions of the 20th and 21st centuries were ever invented?

Pascal believed that we humans are distracting-seeking machines. In a published collection of his notes, known today as *Pensees* (French for "Thoughts") he noted,

> "The only thing which consoles us in our troubles is diversion, and yet it is the greatest trouble of all. For it is chiefly that which prevents us from thinking [about] ourselves... But diversion beguiles us, and brings us at last insensibly to death."39

Distractions, intentional or otherwise, make two distinct claims on you. The first is that someone wants you to make their priorities your priority. The second is that the distraction should remain in your thinking for as long as possible. To borrow a term from our usage of laptops, the distraction should be a part of the wallpaper of your thoughts.

An ancient example of this is found in the Old Testament book of Exodus. As chapter 5 unfolds, you find that Moses has told the Israelites of God's concern for them and His plan to liberate them from slavery in Egypt. Clearly, this should have been of great encouragement to them.

However, the beneficiary of that slave labor, the Pharaoh, sought to crush this. He developed a strategy to both discourage the Israelites and re-focus their attention on his priority. This involved the daily quota of brick production required from the Israelites. Pharaoh issued a strange and seemingly self-defeating edict.

> *You [foremen] are no longer to supply the people with straw for making bricks; let them go and gather their own straw. But require them to make the same number of bricks as before; don't reduce the quota. (Exodus 5:7-8)*

Implementing this edict could seriously delay his projects. Yet, it was issued with a specific purpose.

> *[The Israelites] are lazy; that is why they are crying out, 'Let us go and sacrifice to our God.' Make the work harder for the men so that they keep working and pay no attention to lies. (Exodus 5:8-9)*

Pharaoh demanded more of the Israelites than their slave labor. He also demanded their focused attention – on himself and on his building projects. He considered that his building projects were not only his priority but must be the priority of the Israelites as well.

Most likely, your distractions are not as burdensome as those the enslaved Israelites faced so many centuries ago. Yet, whether a distraction is painful or pleasant, self-inflicted, or inflicted by others, the net effect is that a distraction takes your mind away from its proper focus. In other words, a distraction is a way for you to forget something, or someone, more important.

The Capsule

The God who made you knows how easily your mind can wander. As a result, you will find repeated commands throughout the Bible for you to resist forgetfulness and practice the skill of remembering. One reason for biblical meditation is that it serves to keep Christ in our thoughts. Nathanael Ranew keenly observed, "The neglect of this duty, is a denying of his [Christ's] right and royalty over my thoughts."[40]

The Bible's commands to remember take several forms:
- Remembering God
- Remembering Christ
- Remembering what God has done for His people throughout time
- Remembering what God has done for you

Remembering God

The God who created you knows your limitations. He knows the limitations imposed simply by your physical framework. He also knows those which restrict you due to your fallen, sinful human nature which you share with all other children of Adam. God knows that without an ongoing focus on Him on your part, your focus and priority will drift from being God-centered to being focused on anyone or anything else.

Remembering God is not something passive. It will not happen by default. As already discussed, so many things seek to deflect your attention elsewhere. Such remembrance is a discipline which must be actively developed. Fortunately, Scripture lays out several commands and patterns for you to follow to remember God.

One book which contains an abundance of these commands and patterns is the book of Deuteronomy. The title "Deuteronomy" comes from the Greek term for "Second Law." It is the narrative of Moses recounting to the Israelites a summary of their forty-year wanderings and God's specific instructions as they are on the verge of entering the Promised Land. In the English Standard Version translation of Deuteronomy, there are thirteen specific commands to remember God and eight to not forget what God had done for His people.

In the text of Deuteronomy 8, Moses recounted God's kindnesses to the Israelites during those prior forty years. This retelling of those blessings acted as the background for the command and warning found in Deuteronomy 8:18-19.

> *You shall remember the LORD your God, for it is he who gives you power to get wealth, that he may confirm his covenant that he swore to your fathers, as it is this day. And if you forget the LORD your God and go after other gods and serve them and worship them, I solemnly warn you today that you shall surely perish.*

In the midst of the material prosperity which the Israelites would enjoy in the Promised Land, they were warned, before entering the Land, to remember their God, from whose hand they received these blessings. The lesson applies to you as well. Even those who are among the economically poorest in western societies today are remarkably materially prosperous by the standards of other nations on Earth. Like those Israelites of so many centuries ago, you are told to remember God and not forget Him in the midst of your material blessings.

The Capsule

Reading and re-reading Scripture on an ongoing basis is a great means by which to remember God and not forget Him. Scripture also gives you commands and patterns which rely on your ability to see something that causes you to keep God in your memory. They serve as reminders without words.

Blue Tassels and a Pillar of Stones

Many people have photographs scattered throughout their homes. Some are on shelves or fireplace mantles or affixed to a wall. They serve as reminders of loved ones and special times. It's not that you need these photos to remember these beloved individuals and special times. But they do serve a purpose; they are visual prompts that draw your attention to special people and special times. I do this myself.

On the desks in my home office, I keep several photographs. One is of Julie and me when we got married. Another is of our family, twenty-six years later, on the day that my older son and his wife were married. There is a picture of my grandchildren. Upon entering my office, one sees a photo of Julie and me, standing in Parliament Square in London with Big Ben behind us as we celebrated our 25th anniversary. It's not that I can't remember those faces and special times without those photos. Yet, they serve, throughout my day, as welcome reminders of special times with those I love.

The people of ancient Israel, during the time of Moses, did not have photography. Yet, their God called them to set up reminders of Him so that they would not forget the Lord. One of these reminders was so designed that they would always have it with them. In Numbers chapter 15, the Lord commanded Moses to do the following:

Speak to the people of Israel, and tell them to make tassels on the corners of their garments throughout their generations, and to put a cord of blue on the tassel of each corner. And it shall be a tassel for you to look at and remember all the commandments of the LORD, to do them, not to follow after your own heart and your own eyes, which you are inclined to whore after. So you shall remember and do all my commandments, and be holy to your God. (Numbers 15:38-40)

Almost forty years later, a new generation of the people of God was about to enter the land which God had promised to them. Their new leader, Joshua, was given a command to ensure that the people would not forget the God who brought them to this new land. After crossing a flood-stage Jordan River which had been miraculously stopped to allow the people to enter on dry ground, God gave instructions to Joshua.

Take twelve men from the people, from each tribe a man, and command them, saying, 'Take twelve stones from here out of the midst of the Jordan, from the very place where the priests' feet stood firmly, and bring them over with you and lay them down in the place where you lodge tonight. (Joshua 4:2-3)

Why would God order Joshua to do this?

[That] this may be a sign among you. When your children ask in time to come, 'What do those stones mean to you?' then you shall tell them that the waters of the Jordan were cut off before the ark of the covenant of the LORD. When it passed over the

> *Jordan, the waters of the Jordan were cut off. So these stones shall be to the people of Israel a memorial forever. (Joshua 4:6-7)*

Remembering, and not forgetting God, is critical to your relationship with Him. In His kindness, He provided, not just for the ancient Israelites but for you today as well, the means of keeping Him in your memory. Knowing you as He does, He provided those means through His instructions in the Bible. Those means include not only the written text but the use of visual prompts as well.

Remembering Christ

While it is important for you to remember God, the One who is Father, Son, and Holy Spirit, followers of Christ are also instructed in Scripture to specifically remember the Lord Jesus. Perhaps the best-known command for Him to be remembered by His people was spoken by the Lord Himself on the night of the Last Supper. In what has also come to be known as the Lord's Supper, Christ commanded His followers, then and those in the future, in this manner:

> *And he took bread, and when he had given thanks, he broke it and gave it to them, saying, "This is my body, which is given for you. Do this in **remembrance** of me." (Luke 22:19)* Emphasis added.

The purpose of the Capsule is to assist you in your devotional life as you practice it *individually.*

While the importance of participating in this remembrance of Christ in a worthy manner is vital to growing in Christ, note that it is practiced with others, not individually. As a result, I will defer further commentary on the Lord's Supper to others.

Note the command from the Apostle Paul to *"Remember Jesus Christ, risen from the dead, the offspring of David, as preached in my gospel"* *(2 Timothy 2:8).* Paul gave this command to Timothy, a next-generation preacher of the Gospel. It's important for you to note that this command was originally delivered to a Christian minister. Unfortunately, it's not impossible for even a minister to not remember Jesus. There are times when the desire to serve the Lord can overtake the desire to know Him better. This is a caution for all believers, whether in full-time ministry or in some other form of service to the Lord. Busyness can obscure your relationship with Christ. You need to remember that you must remember Christ.

Remembering Christ includes remembering His words. There is a pattern in the Gospel accounts in which words spoken by the Lord Jesus are remembered by His disciples at a later time. Implicitly, the disciples not only remember that He said something but became enabled to understand why He said it.

One example is found in the account of Jesus overturning the merchants' tables within the Temple in Jerusalem. When challenged about His authority to do this,

> *Jesus answered them, "Destroy this temple, and in three days I will raise it up." The Jews then said, "It has taken forty-six years to build this temple, and will you raise it up in three days?" But he was speaking about the temple of his body. When therefore he was raised from the dead, his disciples **remembered** that*

> *he had said this, and they believed the Scripture and the word that Jesus had spoken. (John 2:19-22)* Emphasis added.

As you read the Scriptures, particularly the New Testament, you have the privilege of having the words of Christ recorded for your spiritual benefit which aids you in your remembrance of Him. Those words are expanded on in the Gospel accounts, the historical narrative known as the Acts of the Apostles, as well as letters written by apostles such as Paul, James, Peter, and John. There were instances in which the Lord Jesus interpreted His own parables (Matthew 13:10-23,36-43). He even contributed letters dictated to seven of the churches in what is now modern-day Turkey (Revelation chapters 2,3).

In fact, the reading of all of Scripture gives you the opportunity to remember Christ. Luke points this out in his Gospel account. The events of Luke 24 happened on the day of Jesus' rising from the dead. While traveling with two of His disciples (who didn't yet realize this was Christ), Luke says of the Lord that *"beginning with Moses and all the Prophets, he interpreted to them in all the Scriptures the things concerning himself" (Luke 24:27).* Clearly, Christ is referred to throughout the New Testament. The passage from Luke shows that Christ is also referred to throughout the Old Testament as well. Be mindful that as you read the entirety of the Bible, remember to read the text with an eye toward seeking out how Christ applies to what you are reading.

Remembering what God has done for his people

When you read Scripture, note the passages that discuss what God has done for His people. Paul, in writing to believers in the city of Corinth, summarized what happened to the people of Israel in the time of Moses. The experiences of those Israelites had instructive benefit for the Corinthians, centuries after they happened. They instruct us today as well. *Now these things happened to them as an example, but they were written down for our instruction, on whom the end of the ages has come (1 Corinthians 10:11).* Recalling the sins and errors of others as found in the Bible can also serve as useful instruction for you.

Many of the Psalms recall what God did for his people. Psalm 105:5 points this out so simply. *"Remember the wondrous works that he has done, his miracles, and the judgments he uttered."*

Psalms 78, 105, and 106 provide a summarized history of God's workings among His people. It would be wise of you to not simply read such Psalms as merely an historical account of a people who lived long ago and far away. These too were written for your benefit, to know that God works in real human history, not only then and there, but also here and now.

A reading of the entire New Testament will show you the unmerited favor that God has shown (and continues to show) to His people. The New Testament text centers on what the Lord Jesus did in His death, resurrection, and ascension to Heaven to pay for the sin debt of His people and restore them to right relationship with God. Reflect on what Christ did. Keep it in your memory. This is a key way to remember what God has done for His people.

The Capsule

Remembering what God has done for you

Clearly, God has guided and cared for His people throughout human history. There are times when God's people today, those who have trusted in Christ alone for life here and in eternity, need to be reminded of God's love, care, and concern for them individually. Psalm 23, 73, and 139, for example, are not written in the collective voice to a group of people. They are written with the voice of an individual in mind. This should be of great comfort to you. God knows us, individually, and by name. He knows every move you make, every thought, every word you utter (see Psalm 139:2-4). Because this is true, you can pray with the Psalmist, *"I am continually with you; you hold my right hand. You guide me with your counsel, and afterward you will receive me to glory."* *(Psalm 73:23-24)*

Several years ago, I was challenged with the following question: "While you really believe what the Bible says about God, do you really believe what the Bible says about you?" Perhaps, your view of God is as accurate as your imperfect human nature allows. Yet, while that view might be accurate, that is no guarantee that you will see yourself in the way that God intends.

Allow me to challenge you with a further question; Who are you? If asked this same question, many of those around you might give a variety of answers. Some may identify themselves by their first and last names, others may do so by their ethnicity, political affiliation, or religious ideology. Undoubtedly, there would be many more answers as well.

For the one who is in Christ, though, the primary answer should be "I am in Christ." This doesn't destroy other identities by which we are known in this life. However, those identities will fade away as a follower of Christ leaves this world and enters into eternity. Identity in Christ is eternal. Being in Christ is your highest and truest identity. As you seek to set up ways to remember God in Christ, I recommend that you also set up ways for you to remember who you are in Christ and what He has done, is doing, and will do for you.

Tokens of Remembrance

When you visit a tourist attraction, it is quite common to have numerous stores nearby that sell souvenirs. Souvenirs can take the form of just about anything from coffee mugs and T-Shirts to sweatshirts and caps; all stamped with the location of the tourist attraction. When Julie and I were in London, the souvenir stores we visited were loaded with replicas of the Big Ben clock tower or some creative use of the Union Jack on items such as pens, notebooks, or playing cards.

The word "souvenir" is a French word which means "to remember." It is a good word for us to keep in mind, especially if we can disconnect it from buying a cheap, plastic trinket with a limited shelf-life. There are souvenirs that can promote your ability to remember God and what He has done for you. I brought back some souvenirs from a trip to Canterbury, England. This village is the site of Canterbury Cathedral as well as the ruins of Saint Augustine's Abbey, the site of one of the earliest Christian missions to England dating back to the late 6th century.

Stephen Langton, the Archbishop of Canterbury in the early 13th century, who came up with the modern chapter divisions of the Bible which we use today, walked the aisles of the cathedral. Saint Pancras Chapel, the ruins of which still stand on the grounds of Saint Augustine's Abbey, was used for Christian worship dating back to the very early 7th century.41

God has been working for centuries with the people of England on these sites. It is difficult, as an American from the Midwest, to comprehend this historical time scale. A building in the Detroit area which dates back 150 years is considered very old. In Canterbury, 150 years ago is recent history. These souvenirs I brought back are reminders to me that real human beings were living God-honoring lives, under times and circumstances that I could barely imagine.

A souvenir is not necessarily something that you need to bring home from another place. Perhaps a special souvenir may be a family Bible which you have inherited. It might be a journal written by a beloved family member or friend. While not on the scale of history of Canterbury, these souvenirs can be a reminder of God's faithfulness in the lives of those who have gone before you.

Remembrance is not passive. It requires discipline. A practice which I've started for myself was a current-day version of the blue tassel mentioned earlier. I've been in the habit of carrying a blue-barreled pen with me to serve the same purpose as the blue tassel did in the time of Moses. When I look at the pen, I am reminded of God.

The discipline of remembering requires effort. It may be helpful for you set up remembrances of the goodness, kindness, and mercy which God has shown to you during your time on Earth. There may be people who have helped in your walk of faith whose pattern of life you do not want to forget. There may be certain events that have had an impact on your life. Ask yourself who and what you want to remember and not forget. Ask yourself, then, what you can do to ensure these don't get lost in the mists of forgetfulness.

Let me offer a personal example of setting up a practice of remembrance. I set aside every December 4th as "Regeneration Day." It is an intentional reminder of the day that I came to faith in 1984. Ironically, I chose this date since I do not remember the exact date it happened. For me, it is important to remember the event even if I cannot recall the exact date.

Memories of the Future

Typically, remembrance has a view to the past attached to it. However, it has a future dimension as well. Monuments are built so that future generations will not forget someone or an event from the past. In Joshua 22:10-34, you find the account of a replica of the Lord's altar built by the Israelites who settled on the east side of the Jordan River. Fearing that this natural barrier might lead to a future division in the nation of Israel, the replica altar was not a lapse into false worship. It was intended as a reminder for future generations. The explanation offered in verse 24 provided a simple reason: *"...we did it from fear that in time to come your children might say to our children, 'What have you to do with the LORD, the God of Israel?'"* Remembrance provides an interesting link between the past and the future.

Numerous Christmas carols serve the same function. In western culture, the celebration of the Christmas season is a time that brings back memories of past Christmases and those with whom you celebrated them. Christmas carols are especially good at triggering those memories of the past. Yet, many of the classic Christmas carols provide us with

The Capsule

"memories of the future." They are, words remembered from earlier in your life. However, they point to a yet future time. Consider a carol such as *"It Came Upon the Midnight Clear"*.

For lo, the days are hast'ning on,
by prophets seen of old,
When with the ever-circling years
Shall come the time foretold,
When the new heav'n and earth shall own
The Prince of Peace their King,
And the whole world send back the song
Which now the angels sing.42

Another nineteenth-century carol from our past, *"Away in a Manger"* brings back memories of the past but also of the future. Its last stanza is a prayer and a look ahead.

Be near me Lord Jesus I ask Thee to stay
Close by me for ever, and love me, I pray.
Bless all the dear children in Thy tender care,
And fit us for heaven, to live with Thee there.43

In remembrance, we look not just to the past. We look to the future as well.

Apollo-era remembrance

Remembrance was a part of the flights of the Apollo astronauts on their missions of lunar exploration. The memory of the assassinated 35th President of the United States, John F. Kennedy was ever-present in the American space program during the 1960s. His 1961 challenge to the nation was arguably the driving force for getting men to the Moon and returning them safely before the year 1970.

Countless thousands involved with the American space effort took to heart their remembrance of Kennedy's challenge. From the time of that challenge, the United States went, in eight years, from having less than one hour of manned spaceflight to safely landing two men on the surface of the Moon and returning them safely to Earth.

There is a second remembrance of note. It wasn't known at the time but was revealed to the general public much later. In the summer of 1971, David Scott, the commander of the Apollo 15 mission, left a memorial on the surface of the Moon. The memorial was an abstract figure of a person cast in aluminum. Aluminum is a metal which can withstand the cycles of harsh heat and cold which occur during a lunar month. The memorial was simply entitled "Fallen Astronaut." It was placed face down and left behind in the lunar soil. The Fallen Astronaut was accompanied by a roster of names, as a remembrance of the American astronauts and Soviet cosmonauts who died in the line of duty.

The remembrance of those early space travelers who died in service was quite an appropriate gesture by David Scott and the crew of Apollo 15. We, who engage in our own Capsule practice here on Earth, are called to remembrance as well. The one we remember died in His service to His people. Better yet, He rose back to life for His people as well. Ultimately, our remembrance of Christ does not end with His death but also His rising from the dead and ascending to Heaven. Our remembrance is of the One who described Himself the best: *"Fear not, I am the first and the last, and the living one. I died, and behold I am alive forevermore."* *(Revelation 1:17-18)*

Takeaways

1. Recognize that we live in a distraction culture as well as being distraction seekers.
2. Set up "souvenirs" as tokens of remembrance to keep you focused on Christ.
3. If you are in Christ, remember your identity is in Christ. Ask yourself often: "Who am I?"
4. Remembrance isn't just focused on the past; Remembrance points to the future as well.
5. When it comes to remembering Christ and all He has done for you, as always, be creative.

Chapter 8

The Need for Focused Solitude

"...[those] who understood the times..." 1 Chronicles 12:32

In this book, I have examined several practices and mindsets which can be useful in your devotional time with Christ. The Apollo astronauts who were the lone occupants of those capsules that orbited the Moon, accomplished much in that time of enforced solitude. Similarly, you too will benefit from time in solitude with God in the following ways: The Presence Chamber, where you meet with your divine monarch and interact with Him; The Chapter House, where you seek to place into order the tasks of your life, including following a rule of faith; being open to the benefits of analog or digital technology in seeking solitary time with Christ; reading, in which the reflections of others can become our reflections; taking the Capsule outdoors, in which the mindset of being alone meets with the great outdoors; remembrance, so that you never forget Christ or who you are in Him.

This book is intended to encourage you to pursue these, as well as other practices that develop from your own creativity. I encourage you to do these alone. Not only will you benefit, but those with whom you interact on a daily basis, will also benefit from you as a result.

The question naturally follows, "How can my time in solitude be of benefit to others?" Solitude, in this context, is not escapism from others. It is not a call to live life as a hermit in permanent isolation from family, friends, and neighbors. However, it is following a practice, as mentioned in Chapter

The Capsule

1, which recognizes the need for a cycle between solitude and re-engagement with others.

This kind of solitude is pursued by remembering what kind of a creature you really are. Like every other human, you are a physical being made in the image of God (Genesis 1:27). You are not simply matter; You are not simply spirit. The aspects of your spiritual life, physical being, emotions, and mental health combine to make you the person you are. True solitude impacts your spiritual side but not only your spiritual side. It affects the totality of who you are. True solitude in Christ should be a reset for your whole person. This is important to remember; especially considering the digital technology era we live in and how we are impacted by it, often in ways no one could predict even a generation ago.

In reading the Gospels, you will note the pattern of the Lord Jesus' cycle of entering into solitude and then re-engaging with others. He spent time with the crowds and would then leave those crowds to spend time alone with His Father. If the Lord of Glory needed to pray, how much more do we need to pray?

In Mark 1:29-33, the text shows how the Lord Jesus performed a number of healings at the home of Simon Peter and Andrew. After leaving a Sabbath service, the Lord started the healings with Peter's mother-in-law. Later, that evening, others were brought *"who were sick or oppressed by demons. And the whole city was gathered together at the door." (Mark 1:32-33).*

After what was a busy night, the Lord did not "sleep in." He understood the priority of prayer and communing alone with His Father in Heaven. Mark writes, *"And rising very early in the morning, while it was still dark, he departed and went out to a desolate place, and there he prayed"* (Mark 1:35). Jesus knew that this time in solitude would not simply happen by itself. It required purposeful effort. A lesson to be taken from this passage reminds you that allowing others to set your agenda is rather unwise. It is a reminder to us to recognize our times and how to redeem them for God's glory.

A Watershed Moment

A watershed can be defined as "The ridge or crest line dividing two drainage areas" 44 The Rocky Mountains of the western United States provide a wonderful example. Rain or snow that falls only a few inches away from each other on opposite sides of the watershed line will eventually drain in two different bodies of water. Both are bound for oceans. One goes west to the Pacific. The other travels east to the Atlantic

This same term is applied to momentous events in life or in history. It is defined as: "an important point of division or transition between two phases, conditions, etc.:"45 I believe that the world is currently going through such a watershed time in the advance of digital technology. This historical watershed is defining not only how you live but how you think and interact with others as well as yourself.

Sometimes, it is clear when historic events are about to unfold. Winston Churchill correctly understood this in the 1930s when he warned England of the danger that Adolph Hitler would pose to his nation as well as the world. In the United States in the late 1850s, it was becoming clear that the nation was headed for a civil war. The war's arrival in 1861 was met with sadness. It was met with unrealistic hopes that the conflict would be very short-lived, although its arrival surprised few.

However, there seem to be times when, for lack of a better term, history sneaks up on you. A prime example is the COVID 19 pandemic which began in late 2019 and spread throughout the world in a matter of months. At the time of this writing, it is still playing a major role in world affairs. This "sneaking up" can happen with the introduction of new ideas and new inventions. Often, there is no recognition that they will be history-making and life changing. As the years move along, there are times when the implications of those new ideas and inventions slowly become apparent.

An example of this occurred in mid-15th century Europe with the invention of a movable-type printing press by Johannes Gutenberg (c.1400 – 1468). Prior to Gutenberg, producing a book in Europe required hand copying a previously existing copy. Thus, only wealthy people could afford the cost of having a copyist produce such a text. With the invention of the printing press in Europe (note that versions of movable-type printing existed centuries earlier in China and Korea) 46, a book could be produced more quickly. They were far more affordable than a hand copied counterpart. An added benefit was the ability to print a book with far fewer errors than happened when a text was hand copied.

Gutenberg could not have imagined the broad implications of his invention on life in Europe. It is safe to say that among the revolutionary effects of his work was the creation of printed New Testament texts in Greek. Using those texts, scholars and theologians noted the differences between them and the Latin Vulgate, (the official Bible version of the Roman Catholic Church then and now). The cry of those

Renaissance-era scholars was "ad fontes" (go back to the original sources). One result? Eighty years after Gutenberg's invention, the use of the printing press led to the launch of the Protestant Reformation.

A similar revolution began in the 1970s when Steve Jobs and Steve Wozniak created the first Apple computers. Those early devices were seen by many as simply an interesting toy for hobbyists. In the late 1970s, few people would have imagined that personal computers would one day become commonplace throughout the world. In 1977, Ken Olsen, the founder of Digital Equipment Corporation, reflected the mindset of the time when he said, "There is no reason anyone would want a computer in their home."[47]

Fast forward in time to the third decade of the 21st century. Millions of people in the decades since 1977 could have told Olsen why they want a computer in their home or automobile. Similar to the way that the invention of the European printing press had unforeseen effects, the same holds true for the digital revolution of the late 20th and early 21st centuries. Like the printing press, the benefits were also attended by unexpected consequences.

The digital revolution has improved the lives of others in so many ways. I am grateful to live in a time in which I've watched these benefits develop and unfold. As a "digital immigrant" (a term coined by Marc Prensky in 2001)[48], I have vivid memories of the pre-digital world and the transition to the digital world of today. This is unlike the "digital natives" born after 1985. They have no living memory of a time without the internet or digital devices. I've learned to recognize and appreciate those benefits with my living memories of "before" and "after."

The Capsule

Two unforeseen effects will be discussed here. As you will see, these concerns are intertwined. One effect is the enlarged capacity for distraction. The second is hyper-connectedness.

Distraction is nothing new. It features prominently in the discussion of remembrance in Chapter 7. Distraction was not invented in the digital age. Radio and television carried that potential (and often, in actuality) in a pre-digital age. In 1990, as the digital world which we know today was beginning to emerge, the average number of hours of television watched per day in American households was just short of 7 hours.49

What is new is the expanded capacity for distraction to which digital-era devices "open the door." As digital devices have changed over time, one dominating trend was building greater mobility into these devices. Consider this from the perspective of the development of the earliest home computers to what is currently available in the third decade of this century. In the 1990s, the earliest home computers that were able to access the internet were large devices which sat on, or just under a desk. Internet access came through a dial-up modem. When you were online, so was your landline telephone as it was busy carrying the signal.

As time went by, the desktop was slowly replaced by the laptop. While laptops are still common (being much lighter than their early counterparts), many of their functions can be found in smart phones and smart tablets. They are easier to carry and no longer need to be tethered to one physical location.

To be fair, the mobility of smart devices can be of tremendous benefit to its users. One early reason for cell phone purchases was to be able to call for help from your car if you became stranded. In current times, being able to text information or call someone from a portable device can be quite a blessing. Let's face it. Having the ability to text or call my wife with a question about our grocery list, while I'm still at the store, has been quite a time-saver.

However, without a purposeful, disciplined approach to using your smart device, that device's mobility can enable further distraction. Again, using the example from the early 1990s, consider that playing that "just one more" game of solitaire on your desktop computer required you to be tethered to your desk. Three decades later, distraction is now fully mobile. Now, you can play many "just one more" games of solitaire sitting in your car, waiting in line at a restaurant, at the beach, or hundreds of other places. In other words, almost no place today is out of the range of internet access. Among the drawbacks is that almost no place today is out of range of smart device distraction.

Quite a bit has changed since the 1990s. This is more than simply taking your 1990's-era desktop computer and shrinking it to carry it around. Email, texts, social media, and videos add to the potential for distraction. It is no secret that algorithms developed and used by social media platforms and video sites are set up to reflect and anticipate your interests while you are online. All of this is done with the purposeful intent of keeping you online (i.e., distracting you) as long as possible.

A second unintended effect of the digital revolution is hyper-connectedness. This derives from a re-thinking of what it means to be in community. In the pre-digital era, there was an implicit assumption that the concept of community involved the idea of physical community. In retrospect, we can see that there were already aspects of thinking in terms of non-physical community. Letter writing and the use of the telephone to maintain contact over long distances are two examples. Yet, those practices were never thought, at the time, to be a replacement for physical community.

Technology and the circumstances of history force us to ask the following: In what sense is a virtual community an actual community? The COVID-19 pandemic of the early 2020s was a large, driving force behind a redefinition of community. Many around the United States and around the world were placed into a position of working online for extended periods of time. (At the time of this writing, I have been working almost exclusively from home for well over two-and-a-half years). Online conferencing offers a digital alternative for office meetings, family get-togethers, and group gatherings.

Is a virtual community an actual community? Some will answer with an emphatic "no." I've witnessed a few examples of this. In these examples, virtual does not mean "alternative." It means "non-existent." A prospective member of our Tuesday night Bible Study indicated that he didn't want to meet online for the study but rather wanted "authentic fellowship." Years ago, I started to bring a Bible e-reader to the Bible Studies at my old church. On one occasion, when I was reading the text from the screen, one of the class participants held up her paper and ink copy of the Bible and proudly proclaimed that she was using a "real Bible."

Is a virtual community an actual community? Some will answer "yes." There are aspects of community that can be maintained in a virtual community, especially if physical community isn't an option. In the case of my Tuesday night Bible study, I'm grateful for the online conferencing app that allows us to meet, to see and hear each other despite being physically separated by many miles. It has even opened up opportunities that couldn't occur if we only met physically. One of our members was helping a family member in Georgia for several weeks and could only attend the study virtually. Another member lives over fifty miles from our old physical meeting site. He simply could not attend at all if we met only in person. While virtual gatherings might be considered a "second best" to face-to-face meetings, they do offer options and opportunities not afforded by physically gathering.

Telephone calls, along with other kinds of audio and video communication, are forms of real-time communication. In other words, you are interacting with someone instantaneously. Texts, emails, and social media messaging offer ways to communicate with staggered levels of response time. You could respond to a text five minutes – or five days – after you receive it.

Using my digital immigrant memories of the pre-digital era, I recall the customary boundaries on telephone usage. While there were always occasions for the unexpected phone call in the middle-of-the-night such as a medical emergency, typically one would never make an unexpected phone call after 9:00 p.m.

In looking back at a pre-digital world, a built-in assumption, which I think is easier to recognize now than it was then, was an assumption of being unavailable for some periods of time. In pre-digital times, there were times when television stations "signed off" for the night. For about three or four hours every day in the very early morning, a television station would stop transmitting. To a digital native, the idea of a television station "signing off" each day for a few hours would be as odd as seeing the sun rise in the west.

A strange shift in the mindset about what it means to be in community has occurred when it comes to the use of social media, texts, and emails. Tools intended for staggered communication are being re-purposed by many into real time tools. What this means is that there are those who never "sign-off." For them, there is the implicit assumption that they must make themselves available for whenever a next posting might be received, regardless of the time of day or night. Often, this doesn't reflect an attitude of resentment but a sense of a deep-seated fear. It is the "Fear of Missing Out" (FOMO).

This state of hyper-connectedness has been written about by Jean Twenge. Doctor Twenge is a psychologist who has been researching trends across generations. Her research led to some startling findings. In her 2017 article *"Have Smartphones Destroyed A Generation?"*, Twenge noted the following about those born between 1995 and 2012.

> Psychologically, however, they are more vulnerable than Millennials were: Rates of teen depression and suicide have skyrocketed since 2011. It's not an exaggeration to describe [this generation] as being on the brink of the worst mental-health crisis in decades. Much of this deterioration can be traced to their phones.[50]

Elsewhere in the same article, she writes,

> What happened in 2012 to cause such dramatic shifts in behavior? It was after the Great Recession, which officially lasted from 2007 to 2009 and had a starker

effect on Millennials trying to find a place in a sputtering economy. But it was exactly the moment when the proportion of Americans who owned a smartphone surpassed 50 percent.51

In an address to the United States Military Academy in January of 2020, Twenge observed,

> "So many other causes of mental health issues and depression or happiness are out of our control," she said. "We can't control the genes we are born with. We can't control the bad stuff that happened to us in the past. But we can control what we do with our free time. We can think more mindfully about how we use that time. So, we can talk in person instead. That's good for mental health. It is also good for social skills."52

Jean Twenge is careful not to say that smartphones have caused the teen mental health crisis recognized as starting in 2012. However, she does make a strong correlation between heavy smartphone usage and compromised mental health.

Western culture is rapidly embracing technology-driven habits that can pose dangers to how we think. As this gets closer to being accepted as normal, how could practicing the Capsule help you avoid adopting those habits so you can be of benefit to yourself and others? That will be the core of the discussion in the next chapter.

Takeaways

1. Times of solitude in the Capsule supply you with times to reset your whole person (spiritual, physical, emotional, and mental).
2. You live in a momentous time in history. The rapid rise and prevalence of digital technology has created an historical watershed between the pre-digital and digital eras.
3. Distractions are not unique to the digital age; today, they simply have greater mobility.
4. The benefits of virtual community can be blunted by occasions to seek distraction and maintain hyper-connectedness.
5. The effects on mental health through the misuse of smart technology have already been documented in research findings.
6. Be prepared, as you read the next chapter, to ask yourself, "How can my time in solitude be of benefit to others?"

Chapter 9

For the Sake of Others

"...you shall love your neighbor as yourself" Leviticus 19:18

Two big ideas have been discussed in this book concerning this era and its circumstances. The first is that the types and frequency of distractions are greater than ever. The second is that society's trend toward being hyper-connected using smart devices is resulting in increased, real-life disconnection with others.

Though these things are happening on this scale for the first time in human history, our deepest aspirations remain the same. First, we seek emotional calm. Second, we seek clearness and soundness of mind. Third, we desire a healthy body, free from aches and pains. Lastly, we aspire for our souls to be at peace.

The technology of this time has the potential, if misused, to disrupt those four aspirations. I've already discussed the effects on the mental health of the generation that grew up with smartphones. Considering more fragile emotions and the physical effects of worry on the body from the "fear of missing out," it's even more difficult to imagine such a person's soul finding rest.

My concern about the potential misuse springs from the perspective of being a digital migrant. I've known life without and with the level of technology available to you in this third decade of the twenty-first century. Having lived in both worlds, I've seen the benefits as well as the unintended drawbacks of smart technology in this digital age.

The Value of the Capsule in Our Time

At a time like this, I believe that the Capsule mindset can be of great benefit to not only you, but also those you know. As your emotions, mental health, body, and soul experience a reset, those effects on you will be noticed by those around you. You will be able to model a life that others are hungry to find.

It will help here to briefly re-visit what the Capsule is and what it is not. The Capsule is a mindset. It is an approach to your devotional life. It does not supply its content. The true success you will find, should you begin to follow the Capsule mindset, is not the strict adherence to the suggestions which you find here. Rather, it is because of the devotional content and the object of that content that you bring with you into the Capsule.

The object of your devotional content must be Jesus Christ. Every Capsule practice is geared to help you follow the Lord Jesus. Every practice is an encouragement to look to Him and trust Him to adopt you as a child of God. Every practice is intended to help you know that if you trust Him, He will watch over your life, both here and in eternity. As King David reminds us, *"The LORD will guard your going out and your coming in, From this time forth and forever" (Psalm 121:8).*

This must be the core of why you would enter the Capsule. Without Christ, you can do nothing (John 15:1-15). Without Him, the practices of the Capsule are meaningless.

Being Countercultural

Throughout the history of the church, followers of Christ have often been called to be countercultural. This has not been done simply out of a desire to be different or contrary. It stems from a recognition that Christ calls His followers to be light and salt.[53] Light exposes darkness. Salt has been used throughout history as a preservative. Ideally, Christian influence in a society should be that of a preservative in the midst of decay and corruption.

Christians of the early centuries of the church presented to the Roman world ways of thinking and acting which stood in stark contrast to the culture of that time. Believers held that true humility was a virtue and not a character flaw. Sexual ethics were such that it was recognized that hospitable Christians were those who were "free to share his neighbour's table, but never his marriage bed." [54] While called to respect and obey their Roman leaders, believers in Christ understood that the crucified and risen Jesus was truly Lord, not the reigning Caesar.

The countercultural dimension of Christian life throughout church history has been in response to the sins and errors of the particular time and place in which those Christ-followers have been placed. Church history is filled with accounts of those who recognized the sins and errors of their time and fought back. Sadly, it is also filled with accounts of those who gave in and accepted the sins and errors of their culture as simply the way they needed to live life.

There are many ills which the church faithful today address and act to resolve. My focus is on distraction and hyper-connectedness, both of which I believe can be countered through Capsule practice. I believe that if these trends continue and are left unchallenged, they will become the new normal for our culture. I've already discussed the potential for disruption in our society. Such trends could also be destructive of your life in Christ. Solitude, needed for your whole-person health, could be thrown off as a relic of a bygone era. The ability to truly focus on your work or Bible reading or prayer could be endangered by a mindset which sees multi-tasking and distraction-seeking as simply normal.

I cannot stress strongly enough that Capsule practice is intended to be of benefit to you and of benefit to others. An example can be drawn from the instructions given at the start of every plane flight. You are instructed that if a problem develops onboard the plane, the oxygen masks might come down. In that case, those responsible for the care of another are told to put their masks on first. In such a scenario, a well-meaning caregiver might seek to be heroic and put the mask on the other person first. However, such an approach could backfire and the caregiver would succumb to a lack of oxygen before assisting the one in need. Tragically, this would result with no one being helped.

In that sense and to extend the comparison, put your mask on first. Ensure that you are spending focused time in solitude with Christ before telling others about it. As you are built up by this, you can then tell friends and family how your times of focused solitude with Christ have been of so much help to you. Be aware, though, that such behavior may seem more and more strange as time unfolds. This kind of talk will also need a walk.

Don't neglect the time you spend with others. As you continue to meet and interact with them, they will eventually be able to tell that something is different about you. Different in a good way. Be an example for them. Make your practice attractive to them.

One way to be an encouraging role model can be applied in helping many of our fellow believers in Christ when it comes to biblical illiteracy. This concern has been noted by groups such as Ligonier Ministries. Ligonier has conducted several "The State of Theology" surveys over the years. They benchmark what believers in Christ know about the Bible and the beliefs which flow from it. In looking into those findings, it is safe to say that large percentages of church-going Christian believers are ignorant of the basic teachings of the faith. As you model what Bible reading has done for you, be careful of the approach that you use.

Avoid using guilt to pressure them. Almost anyone can be guilted into doing almost anything. . . but only for a short length of time. The message that comes across from the guilt monger is one of duty and drudgery. "You must read your Bible everyday" is the message that comes across, whether implied or stated bluntly. How easily do you embrace drudgery?

The approach I use is that of an invitation to delight. Keep in mind that there is no command in the Bible to read the Bible every day. An honest look at church history will show that prior to the Gutenberg printing press, most Christians either lacked access to a text of the Bible or the ability to read it if they did. Our access to the Bible today is a privilege. Those who can read Scripture and don't are missing out on a great blessing. Isn't it more attractive to invite someone to a banquet than to a time of repeated drudgery?

The Capsule

As you speak to others about your life in Christ and the benefit of spending focused time in solitude with Him, I highly recommend that you speak of this practice as a privilege. Invite those you know to the banquet of Word and prayer. Encourage them to explore practicing the Capsule.

The experience of your time in the Capsule can be used to provide an alternative, a countercultural alternative, to those suffering solitude-deprivation and hyper-connectedness. Like those Apollo astronauts of the 1960s and 1970s, you can tell others of the benefits of "being behind the Moon" in the orbits of your life. Times when nobody can connect with you virtually or in real life, are actually a blessing, not a curse.

Practicing time in the Capsule should be a reminder and a promise to yourself and others of the comforting and trustworthy words of the Lord Jesus, *"Come to Me, all you who labor and are heavy laden and I will give you rest."* (Matthew 11:28)

Takeaways
1. Hyper-distraction and hyper-connectedness could lead to unintended societal consequences. Among these could be an aversion to being alone, an aversion to risk, and a de-emphasis on the importance of independent thought.
2. Faithful Christians, through history, have been countercultural in fighting the evils of their times as well as the challenges.
3. Capsule practice can be a countercultural effort to combat the threat to patterns of thought coming from constant distraction and always being online.
4. As others notice the changes in you, offer them the invitation to solitude with Christ as a time of delight, not drudgery.

Questions for Reflection and Study

1. This book stresses being creative. Think through your current life circumstances. What are some creative ways that you could intentionally set aside times of solitude with God in Christ?

2. What distractions do you face in your current devotional life? What do you do to avoid or minimize those distractions?

3. Make an honest assessment of how you live life. Where have you drifted from living out your ideals? Why? Do you have a plan to get you back on the path to get you closer to living out your ideals?

4. Reflect on how you approach devotions currently. Are they analog, digital or a mixture of both? Ask yourself what could be the benefits or drawbacks of adjusting these? (i.e. too much time listening to podcasts; avoid taking in books using audio books thinking that you can only read a book in print)

5. Reading works from the past can help us see our blind spots in the present. Imagine historians in the 22nd century looking back to our time. What do you think they will find as the cultural blind spots of our time?

6. Meditation (reflection), as referred to in the Bible, can center on either God's written Word or His works in nature. Have you ever done either of these kinds of meditation? If so, how has it impacted you?

7. If you are a follower of Christ, what does it mean to you that your truest identity is in Christ?

8. What are some of the "souvenirs" in your life? What is it about them that sparks a memory within you?

9. For Digital Migrants: Think back to when you purchased your first smart phone. What changes did it make for you in everyday life? What changes did it make for you inwardly (i.e. the way you think; the way you feel)?

10. For Digital Natives: Try to imagine living your life without a smart device (i.e. phone, tablet). This describes daily life only a generation ago. Based on your reflection, ask yourself what are the benefits and the drawbacks of these digital devices to your life?

11. How do you think that times of solitude can be of benefit to you? Consider those you know personally. How can a "re-set" you be of benefit to them?

Endnotes

1
https://www.youtube.com/watch?v=GmN1wO_24Ao
Accessed September 2023

2 space.stackexchange.com

https://space.stackexchange.com/questions/8590/how
-long-did-it-take-for-the-apollo-command-module-to-
orbit-the-moon
Accessed September 2023

3 Cal Newport, *Digital Minimalism,* p.111,
Portfolio/Penguin, New York, 2019.

4 StudyLight.org; Albert Barnes, Commentary on
Matthew 6;
https://www.studylight.org/commentaries/eng/bnb/m
atthew-6.html
Accessed September 2023

5 A.W. Tozer, *The Pursuit of God*, p.4, Christian
Publications, Camp Hill, PA, 1993.

6 Richard Foster, *Celebration of Discipline: The
Path to Spiritual Growth,* p.96, HarperSanFrancisco,
San Francisco, 1978; reprint ed. 1998.

7 monergism.com; Thomas Watson, *Godly Man's
Picture;* p.76
https://www.monergism.com/thethreshold/sdg/watso

---

n/The%20Godly%20Man's%20Picture%20-
%20Thomas%20Watson.pdf
Accessed September 2023

8
https://deovivendiperchristum.wordpress.com/tag/th
omas-brooks/
Accessed September 2023

9 ligionier.org; R. C. Sproul, "What Does "Coram
Deo" Mean?"
https://www.ligonier.org/learn/articles/what-does-
coram-deo-mean
Accessed September 2023

10 Donald S. Whitney;
https://biblicalspirituality.org/wp-
content/uploads/2011/01/Read-One-Page-Per-
Day.pdf
Accessed April 2024

11 https://theopolisinstitute.com/a-history-of-quiet-
times/
Accessed April 2024

12 Kevin DeYoung;
https://clearlyreformed.org/on-the-crushing-guilt-of-
failing-at-quiet-time/
Accessed March 2024

13 Edwards wrote in the preface to his Resolutions:
"Remember to read over these Resolutions once a
week." Found in Elizabeth D. Dodds, *Marriage to a*

Difficult Man, p.201, Audubon Press, Laurel MS, 2003.

14 Elizabeth Barrett Browning, *Aurora Leigh*, p.304, Chapman and Hall, London, 1857.

15 National Air and Space Museum; airandspace.si.edu
 https://airandspace.si.edu/collection-objects/checklist-operations-apollo-11/nasm_A19850133000
Accessed September 2023

16 Nuclino; nuclino.com
https://blog.nuclino.com/the-simple-genius-of-checklists-from-b-17-to-the-apollo-missions#:~:text=Checklists%20proliferated%20to%20every%20corner,gloves%20of%20Armstrong%20and%20Aldrin.
Accessed on September 2023

17 superlibrarymarketing.com

https://superlibrarymarketing.com/2022/07/18/genzmillennialreaders/
Accessed September 2023

18 David McCullough, Interview with NEH chairman Bruce Cole, Humanities, July/Aug. 2002, Vol. 23/No. 4); found at
https://quotes.thefamouspeople.com/david-mccullough-1180.php
Accessed September 2023

19 John MacArthur, Eulogy for R.C. Sproul funeral; found at
https://www.youtube.com/watch?v=Hv_6natO-JY
Accessed September 2023

20 *The Sufficiency of a Standing Revelation,*
Offspring Blackall, H. Hills, London, 1707; found at
https://books.google.com/books?id=NQQ_AAAAc
AAJ&source=gbs_similarbooks Accessed September
2023; A plain, readable text can also be found at
https://quod.lib.umich.edu/e/eebo2/A28280.0001.00
1?rgn=main;view=fulltext
Accessed September 2023

21   seanmcdowell.org
https://seanmcdowell.org/blog/what-is-the-most-
recent-manuscript-count-for-the-new-testament
Accessed September 2023

22 *The Soldier's pocket-book*, Presbyterian Church,
U.S.A. Board of Publication, 1861; found at
https://archive.org/details/soldiers00pres
Accessed September 2023

23 Ibid, p.6.

24 thedecisonlab.com
https://thedecisionlab.com/biases/naive-realism
Accessed September 2023

25 Union Publishing; unionpublishing.org
Michael Reeves, Foreword to Thomas Goodwin's
'The Heart of Christ in Heaven'; found at

https://www.unionpublishing.org/resource/foreword-to-thomas-goodwins-the-heart-of-christ-in-heaven/
Accessed September 2023

26 C.S. Lewis, Introduction to Saint Athanasius, *On the Incarnation*, translated & edited by a religious of CSMV, p.4, Saint Vladimir Seminary Press, Crestwood, 2002.

27 Thomas Watson, A Christian on the Mount: A Treatise Concerning Meditation, p.5; found at https://www.monergism.com/thethreshold/sdg/watson/A%20Christian%20on%20the%20Mount_Thomas%20Watson.pdf
Accessed on September 2023

28 Nathanael Ranew, *Solitude Improved by Divine Mediation,* p.vii-viii, Soli Deo Gloria Publications, Grand Rapids, 2019.

29 desiringGod.org
Charles Haddon Spurgeon found at https://www.desiringgod.org/articles/next-best-to-grace-oxygen.
Accessed on September 2023

30 openingtogod.wordpress.com
https://openingtogod.wordpress.com/2016/07/10/contemplative-walks/ Accessed on September 2023

31 Ranew, pg. v (the page is also listed as A3 at the bottom of the page)

32 Tom Schwanda, *Soul Recreation: Spiritual Marriage and Ravishment in the Contemplative-Mystical Piety of Isaac Ambrose*, Durham theses, Durham University, 2009. Available at https://evangelicalmystics.files.wordpress.com/2010/09/tom-schwanda-soul-recreation2.pdf p.112. Accessed on February 2024

33 Schwanda, p.113.

34 Schwanda, p.116.

35 cleantechnica.com
 https://cleantechnica.com/2022/01/01/the-story-of-the-blue-marble
Accessed September 2023

36 christiantoday.com
 https://www.christiantoday.com/article/theres-a-god-up-there-last-man-on-the-moon-who-marvelled-at-majestic-earth-passes-into-eternity/104018.htm
Accessed September 2023

37 abcnews.go.com
https://abcnews.go.com/Technology/Apollo11Moon Landing/story?id=8124267&page=1
Accessed September 2023

38 thefreedictionary.com
https://www.thefreedictionary.com/attention+economy
Accessed September 2023

39 Blaise Pascal, *Pascal's Pensees or Thoughts on Religion,* translated & edited by Gertrude Burford Rawlings, p.43, The Peter Pauper Press, Mount Vernon, 1900.

40 Ranew, p.14.

41 churchtimes.co.uk
https://www.churchtimes.co.uk/articles/2022/23-september/news/uk/archaeologists-identify-first-english-church-built-by-st-augustine
Accessed September 2023

42 "It Came upon the Midnight Clear" found in THE HYMNAL for Worship and Celebration, Hymn 128, Verse 4, Word Music, Waco, TX, 1986.

43 "Away in a Manger" found in THE HYMNAL, Hymn 157, Verse 3.

44 Dictionary.com
https://www.dictionary.com/browse/watershed
Accessed September 2023

45 Ibid.

46 Literary Hub; lithub.com
M. Sophia Newman, "So, Gutenberg Didn't Actually Invent Printing As We Know It -
On the Unsung Chinese and Korean History of Movable Type"; found at
https://lithub.com/so-gutenberg-didnt-actually-invent-the-printing-press Accessed September 2023

---

47 pcworld.com
Robert Strohmeyer, "The 7 Worst Tech Predictions of All Time"; found at
https://www.pcworld.com/article/532605/worst_tech_predictions.html
Accessed September 2023

48 marcprensky.com
Marc Prensky, "Digital Natives, Digital Immigrants"; found at
https://www.marcprensky.com/writing/Prensky%20-%20Digital%20Natives,%20Digital%20Immigrants%20-%20Part1.pdf
Accessed September 2023

49 The Atlantic; theatlantic.com
Alexis C. Madrigal, "When Did TV Watching Peak?"; found at
https://www.theatlantic.com/technology/archive/2018/05/when-did-tv-watching-peak/561464/
Accessed September 2023

50 The Atlantic; theatlantic.com
Jean M. Twenge, "Have Smartphones Destroyed A Generation?; found at
https://www.theatlantic.com/magazine/archive/2017/09/has-the-smartphone-destroyed-a-generation/534198/
Accessed September 2023

51 Ibid.

52 U.S. Army

Brandon OConnor, "Twenge speaks to Class of 2020 on effects of smartphone usage"; found at https://www.army.mil/article/232490/twenge_speaks_to_class_of_2020_on_effects_of_smartphone_usage Accessed September 2023

53 Matthew 5:13-16

54 Epistle of Diognetus, found in Early Christian Writings, translated by Maxwell Staniforth, p.145, Penguin Books, Middlesex, England, 1987.